FEEDING MY CHILDREN

GLORIA ALCOZER

Book cover design contributor

Maria Teresa Hernandez

FEEDING MY CHILDREN

ISBN: 978-1-73851-70-6-0

BELANDU PUBLISHING

FEEDING MY CHILDREN
First published in paperback in the
United States 2009 under the name
Gloria Alcozer Thomas
Black Freighter Productions

"We draw our strength from the very despair
in which we have been forced to live.
We shall endure." - Cesar Chavez

PROLOGUE

THE OTHER AMERICANS

I never thought over the years that the title of Tejano would create so much confusion for my family and me. Or, that a title identifying one's ethnicity, or lack of it, would define how other ethnic groups identified or related to us as viable human beings.

Tejano can be defined and interpreted in various ways. Two definitions given by the indigenous people in the Southwest area of the United States were: (a). friend and (b). term of endearment. Another interpretation given later by the European settlers who embraced the word, but changed the spelling to Texas, was to identify the geographical region, which included the occupants that settled within the area as 'Texans'.

My ancestors identified with reference (b), but not quite the way the Europeans had intended. They referred to Tejano as an indigenous tribal nation similar to Navajo and Apache; closely related to the Caddo tribal nation. They also strongly opposed any connection to Mexico; racially, culturally and ideologically.

Their descendants later evolved into a nomadic group of people who would pull up stakes and carry their traditions on their back to various states of the union, while maintaining a distinctive language, customs and traditions defined by the individual families and states they settled in.

While growing up in the city of Chicago, I was oblivious to the cultural disputes of my ancestors, and to the past my parents had both adhered to but eventually ran away from. I didn't know my father's father at all. And I knew less of his mother.

When they did visit, I didn't find them to be particularly warm people. So, I didn't feel any obligation to show any affection towards them.

When they were seated in a special area in the living room, I would peek from a corner of the room, or hide behind a sibling so I could stare at them. There was the quick return stare of confirmation that they had noticed me, but it was an ice-cold affirmation unfamiliar to a small child.

As for my mother's parents, I met them for the first time when I was five years of age. I felt an immediate connection with my mother's father. He was warm and loving to me. But I would later make a shocking discovery regarding his relationship with my mother before she left with my dad, of how and why their relationship disintegrated with time.

To understand why my parents had separated from a lifestyle and culture they loved I would have to go back to my parent's tumultuous meeting.

My father was born in Rosenberg, Texas on November 15, 1917 and given the name Eugenio Alcozer. He was married seven times prior to meeting my mother and fathered children in and out of wedlock.

He was a frail man plagued with illness and adversity throughout his life, and was diagnosed with tuberculosis at the age of twelve. His chances of recovery from the disease were grim.

During one of his worst bouts with the illness the hospital physicians advised his parents to have his coffin prepared and ready. But to the amazement of the doctors (but not to the shamans who had nursed him back to health), he miraculously recovered.

(*The shamans, or* "curanderos" as we call them, *used smoke, herbs, ointments and candles—while chanting to the spirit world to heal their patient back to health. This was a common practice that was utilized frequently by my family during various crises of illness).*

The coffin later sat in the back garden of my grandparent's house in Crystal City, Texas for many years. It became the most referred to proof, by my grandparents, of the medical inadequacies of the white man's society.

In 1935, my father, frail and barely literate, was drafted into the Army and stationed at Fort Sheridan in Illinois. It was his first visit to the plains. Impressed with what he saw, he considered that part of the country the new frontier and vowed he would return after his tour of duty. He kept his promise but not until twenty years later.

Within six months of his induction, he was given an honourable discharge based on medical complications, and returned home. He was not a horseman like his father and brothers, and upon returning to Texas, he took to womanizing and the bottle like a fish takes to water.

My father's father stood six feet tall, feared no man and rejoiced that he could physically beat any man into submission. His reputation as a known cattle rustler and for violence made him feared in all the nearby counties.

My grandfather rustled cattle from Mexico and crossed them over the border into Texas, selling the stock to nearby ranchers. He met my grandmother during one of his business ventures. She was living near the Sugarland area in the southeast part of Texas. They married and had my father shortly after.

The Mexican revolution was then in full swing and crossing the border between Mexico and Texas was becoming increasingly dangerous. It was during that time that he decided to leave his cattle rustling days behind and settled in Sugarland with his new wife and baby.

During the years his reputation for being a superior horseman never diminished. He was so renowned, that while filming a movie near Mexico, John Wayne visited my grandfather and solicited his horseman skills. My grandfather refused, but news of the visit by the actor spread far and wide.

Rather than following in my grandfather's footsteps, my father discovered he was a superior poker player in his own right and used his skills for profit. He travelled throughout Texas and Oklahoma winning large booties from the game.

One day during one of his drinking and poker-playing sprees in Oklahoma, he befriended a man whom he had been introduced to several months earlier. One evening, late into a poker game, the man would lose a large amount of money to my father.

Disgraced and desperate, he decided he would recover his losses if he played one more game. He went on to lose all his money, and then made a final desperate wager....he bet his sister, and lost. My mother became my father's eighth wife. She was only thirteen when she left with my father.

My mother's parents were very different from my father's. Her father, also indigenous, was adopted by a childless Spanish couple who were wealthy Texas landowners. Their properties extended across both

Texas and Mexico.

In the late 1890s my grandfather was overseeing the properties of his adoptive parents and travelled frequently to Jalisco, Mexico, on business. In those days there was no such thing as immigration control. Properties were purchased freely regardless of geographical distances.

During one of his business trips in Jalisco he met my grandmother, an uneducated waitress and daughter of poor immigrants from Asturias, Spain. After meeting, they married and stayed in Mexico for two years. My grandmother would come to idolize her husband, forsaking everything to please him, even the children she would later have with him.

Political unrest had begun brewing and political parties were forming quickly. Americans were joining many of those parties and Europeans were also flocking to Mexico to join in the new formed idealist groups as well. Many of them spoke of the radical movement that was taking place in Russia. It was a movement that promised freedom and a classless utopian society.

My grandfather had heard about the movement of Karl Marx, Friedrich Engels and their manifesto. The possibility of Mexico emulating their movement excited him. He was tired of the divisions between the white man and the Indian. If this movement could bring agrarian reform, then he wanted to be a part of it.

In 1909, it was obvious a revolution was at hand in Mexico. My grandfather moved his wife and son to a small town that bordered Mexico and Texas and took an active part in the newly formed ideological movement called Communism. Already disinherited by his parents because of his choices of wife and friends, he decided he had nothing to lose by paying them a visit.

His parents, at first pleased with the long-awaited visit, quickly found it was less than friendly. My grandfather demanded the release of agrarian ownership and that they liberate their peon workers of all debts in Mexico and Texas. Devastated by his betrayal, and lack of loyalty to them, they left Texas and immigrated to Cape Good Hope, South Africa. All communication between them was severed.

> Note: *Upon the death of my grandfather, and during the funeral, an anonymous note and bouquet of flowers arrived from South Africa, extending their condolences to his family; revealing that my grandfather had never been forgotten by them.*

My grandfather became a self-proclaimed visionary, communist, atheist, academic and linguist, fluent in at least five languages. After the war, still very impassioned by the writing of Karl Marx, he left the Southwest on a mission to travel the United States seeking or forming other groups of communist followers.

He travelled to Indiana, and on June 10, 1931, in a small rural town called Tipton, my mother, Anita Martinez, was born.

My grandparents continued travelling across the United States, my grandfather working as a lecturer and my grandmother as a midwife.

In 1935, while very much involved in their ideological pursuits, they decided to send my mother to live with her mother's sister, Natalia in Piedras Negras, Coahuila, Mexico.

They would seldom visit and when they did, their visits were long and emotionally draining for my mother.

Education for non-white European descendants was not compulsory and in some places denied to most. This was not an issue for my grandfather who believed in home schooling. His opinions of the white man's schools were that they were inadequate and brain washing.

When the time came for my mother to return to live with her parents, my grandfather modelled a course of action for lessons. The lessons were intense and sometimes vicious, which caused my mother to shut down, provoking dire repercussions.

His disappointment and frustration at her inability to learn was demonstrated through tirades of violence. He'd accuse her of frivolity, capricious day dreaming and lack of concentration. His impatience would end by slapping her, or hanging her from the ceiling by her arms for long periods of time.

This abuse ultimately left her emotionally scarred and unable to read or write. It wasn't difficult to understand my mother's desire to leave home at thirteen. She needed and wanted to escape.

Before my father won my mother in the poker game, my mother had seen my father on several occasions with her older brother. Through her eyes, she saw a confident and attractive man, with dark skin, large brown eyes, a cleft chin and a wide smile; which she admired. With each encounter she did not hesitate to let him know she liked him.

My father would recount a similar attraction to her. He would tell us how he thought she was the most beautiful girl he had ever seen:

"The first time I saw your mother, she was surrounded by several girls of similar age. They were boarded on the back of a truck on its way to the cotton fields. Her brown wavy hair and skin stood in contrast to the other girls' dark hair and skin. She was also leaner and taller, with almond shaped hazel eyes that twinkled when she smiled. There were several men whistling at her and one guy called her 'star'. I thought to myself, I am going to meet and marry her," he told us proudly.

He later found out why the men called her 'star'. They had come to the conclusion that she resembled a young Susan Hayward. Amused by the comparison he decided he would nickname her Star as well. The name stuck until he died.

After the poker game, my mother's brother tried to negotiate other terms with my father. But my father, a man of few words, made no comment and left. The next day, crossing the road after spending the evening drinking at the local taverna, my mother's brother violently attacked him.

He pushed him to the ground and threatened to kill him should he try to persuade my mother to go with him. My father got up, brushed himself off, smiled and walked away.

Unwilling to give up the idea of collecting his winnings, several days later, he spotted my mother strolling in the park with a few friends. He stopped her and told her she had become the booty of a poker game.

My mother, shocked and devastated by what her brother had done, decided to leave with my father that evening. The following day, my mother's brother, discovering she had gone, swore vengeance for the betrayal of his poker-playing partner.

In Texas, and many other rural states, it wasn't uncommon for young girls to leave home at thirteen. It was especially more frequent within most poor and indigenous families in rural areas. If a young girl left home with her betrothed without ceremony, she was automatically considered married by her family. More often, for many families, the early departure of a family member was welcomed. It meant one less mouth to feed.

Sadly, because this perception of early marriage was shared by most communities, it was not unusual for a rejected suitor to kidnap a young girl, keep her overnight, without her parent's consent, feign intimacy and later wait for her parents to reject her. She would ultimately have to marry her captor.

But my mother's father was not like those indigenous families. He had been brought up in a bourgeois environment. An environment and standards he hated but did not hesitate to exploit. He was knowledgeable of the race laws, and would use the full extent of the law against my father, who he disliked, and referred to as the Indian.

He rounded up local and federal authorities; the Sheriff, Texas Rangers and the Federal Marshal, and demanded they find my mother.

He held in his possession a very important document that he would deliberately use to provoke hostility against my father and heighten their pursuit over state borders. It was her birth certificate, which showed her of “white race.”

The lawmen chased my parents across counties and states, but my father was always two steps ahead of them. At the end, it became a cat and mouse game to determine who was smarter and faster. Their journey across the United States took them to places they never dreamed they would see, or were prepared for.

They crossed the southern borders of states, such as Alabama, Tennessee, Mississippi and Georgia. For my mother, the southern states were another world of cultures and views; too shocking for words.

My mother had heard the stories from her father about men being hung from their necks for being a different race or colour. She thought the stories were made up to frighten her. He told her about the English people; an evil group without morals and values who would steep so low as to murder women and children.

The stories come to life before her eyes. She’d cringe as she came across lynching victims whose bodies swung from trees on ropes along the road as they crossed another state line. They were mostly black, but many were Indian and Mexican as well.

According to my mother, the wealthy landowners in Texas and Mexico were sometimes unfair in imposing their demands on the peon worker. But they never retaliated with such cruelty and violence, at least, not from what she had seen.

In Texas, as she remembered it, "you could go where you wanted, eat in restaurants and go to the town dance. There were never any restrictions."

That wasn't the case outside of Texas. It was another world, a world for her, too frightening to think or talk about. Because of that new awareness of this world, she became conscious of my father's dark skin for the first time.

Yet, she'd say, my father never appeared bothered by any of it. He would laugh and tease her, telling her to wait while he tried to purchase food for them at a local grocery store. She would observe him before he would enter, hanging his head low and not looking at the white man's eyes while talking.

Just before he'd leave, when the owner would look away, he'd smirk then wink at her. Why wasn't he allowed to talk to them directly she'd ask him?

My father would say, "They are stupid. It's better to humour them so they can feel good about themselves." Strangely, as time passed, she would find herself treating her children according to their different shades of colour as well.

During the first years of marriage, as fugitives, my mother worked long days in the fields picking cotton and vegetables. My father, because of his delicate health, could not stand long hours under the sun. Instead, he took odd jobs as an electrician, carpenter or mechanic. There was the odd time when his five brothers would appear at the farm where he was working to give him a hand. During those weekends, they would have barbecues, play the guitar, sing (mostly country and western music), and get drunk.

In 1945, when my mother learned she was expecting her first child, my father decided to join his parents in Crystal City Texas, where his mother was working as the town midwife. He had hoped she could help in the delivery of the baby. My mother was just fifteen. During her stay, her relationship with her mother-in-law became strained. It was obvious my father's mother did not like her, or so my mother said, and the chance of any type of relationship deteriorated. The years passed, and they were never able to warm to each other. Naturally, the stay in Texas was short-lived and my mother returned to working in the fields, this time in Minnesota with her son strapped to her back.

Three more children would follow while they continued to live in rural shacks and work in the fields.

My mother made friends with Swedish farm workers who taught my mother how to cook Swedish meatballs, stuffing, and roast turkey for the annual Thanksgiving dinner. To our delight, she also learned how to bake bread, doughnuts, waffles and cakes.

The Minnesota fields and winters were harsh. So harsh, that my mother pleaded with my father to return to Texas. My father, reluctantly, agreed and prepared to leave with his three sons and daughter, but before returning, my mother would discover again that she was now expecting, at twenty-three, their fifth child.

They stayed in Texas for a little over a year before my father announced that he had decided to move to Illinois. My mother was furious. She didn't want to move anymore. She was tired and yearned to see her parents again. She hadn't seen them since she was thirteen, and she desperately wanted them to forgive her, but my father refused. Ironically, several years later, she would learn that my grandfather had a bought a ranch only an hour away from where they lived in Crystal City.

The exodus to Illinois was a difficult one. There were too many children, five in all, and the probability of finding a place that would accept a family that large was minimal. But my father had a plan. He purchased a trailer, which was more like a four hundred square foot box, moved his family in and parked it on a camp on Higgins Road in Desplaines, Illinois. I was born, in that trailer, in the summer of 1955.

Des Plaines was a rural township outside of Chicago that had just started to boom. With the construction of O'Hare international airport and the start of a new chain of fast food restaurants, called McDonald's, houses and new industries were spreading everywhere. But this wave of new economic growth would not deliver my parents from their poverty.

Their life and hardships remained the same, with my father continuing to work odd jobs and my mother, with babies strapped to her back, working in the fields of Wisconsin.

The years passed with barely enough money to put food on the table. My father earned maybe three dollars a day, that's if there was work to be found. And my mother's wages depended on full baskets of fruit or vegetables which brought only five cents a bushel. A full day's earnings for her could be as low as one dollar. Not enough to feed six children.

There was a glimmer of hope and one source of aid: several years back, through the influence of

Swedish and Polish farm workers, my mother had converted to Catholicism. She became devout, having all her children baptized and attending regular church services.

The local church, recognizing their congregation was made up mostly of farm workers, visited the families regularly with care packages of cheese, clothing and sacks of potatoes and rice. My family were included in these deliveries which lightened the burden of hunger.

One day, to our misery, one of the female Polish farm workers decided to teach my mother how to save money by sewing flour and potato sacks into dresses.

That following summer, my sisters and I would sport fashionable summer dresses that itched something horrible.

By 1960, it was clear the times were changing. Civil unrest in the south and across the nation had begun. My parents, who never forgot the images they saw when driving through the southern states, were uneasy of what lay ahead.

My siblings were getting older, and the trailer was becoming steadily more impractical. Finally, one day my father came home with the exciting news that he had been offered a job as a janitor in a four-unit apartment building in Chicago's west side.

The new job provided a free rental unit, all utilities paid, and a weekly salary, but my father didn't tell my mother everything. She would have to wait until the first night of moving in to find out what he had kept as a secret.

That evening after supper, my father stationed the two eldest sons, with baseball bats, at each end of the apartment, and told them to watch over their sisters and younger siblings while they slept. He also told them that they would have to take special care of the new born baby.

Confused, my brothers did as they were told. The truth emerged within less than three hours, just as it got dark. Giant rats as large as cats leaped out everywhere! They jumped over the children's heads, onto the bed covers and at my brothers.

My father shot at them with a pellet gun and my brothers courageously bashed them with bats. It took my father months before he was able to bring the rats to a controllable level.

My mother never thought she would look forward to another hot summer of work in the fields. But this was a time for desperate measures. When the school term ended, she gathered and packed all her children and took them to work with her in Wisconsin.

She hoped more hands would mean more bushels, more money and a move from the west side.

They worked non-stop. When the summer came to an end, they had earned between them two hundred dollars. It was the most money she had ever grossed.

When she returned to Chicago, she placed the money in a shoe box underneath several wooden floor panels. It would be safe there, hidden away from my father's gambling and drinking.

The money remained hidden for several months, until one day she decided to check the contents of the box. To her horror, she found the rats had gnawed through the box and the money. She cried for days and thought seriously of suicide.

A year later, my father was offered a job that paid seventy-five dollars a week, with a rent-free apartment with utilities included, in a twenty-unit apartment building on Madison and Kedzie. My mother was happy with the arrangement and prayed that this move would be the answer to all her prayers, but it would turn out not to be. The move proved to be one of the biggest challenges to her faith that she had ever confronted.

The apartment unit was comprised of Irish Catholics, Puerto Ricans and Polish residents. The building sat like an island surrounded by an ocean of all Black neighbours, who were demonstrably unhappy with its occupants.

The evenings would pass with rocks and makeshift fire bombs hurled at the windows and back of the apartment unit. My father and my older brothers were constantly on watch guarding the building and its occupants.

The police were unreliable, hardly ever patrolling the area. It was always up to my father and brothers to secure its safety. As time passed it became almost impossible to avoid being confronted with racial slurs and threats of violence. Within less than three months of moving in, my father and brothers had been physically attacked several times.

My mother, fearful again for the safety of her children, demanded we leave Chicago and move back to Texas. My father reassured her that the violence would subside and it would be all over soon, but it wasn't. It got worse...much worse.

The summers continued as always. My father would stay behind in the city while my mother left to work on the fields. She'd take all the children with her, and as before, they worked at her side, saving every penny they made.

In the summer of 1961, the time had finally arrived for my mother to see her parents again. It was an emotional and exciting time for her. My mother's parents, three years earlier, had given up on the United States and decided to purchase a ranch in Mexico.

Feeling anxious, happy, and forgiven, she wanted to make the best impression that she could. So, she bought new dresses for herself, and for the three granddaughters they had never seen. It was a tiny luxury that my father embraced.

She eagerly packed, gave my father instructions on the care of the boys who would stay behind to help their father, and excitedly looked forward to seeing her parents again.

It was a thrilling drive to my grandfather's ranch which was very close to the border between Mexico and Texas. The last few miles felt endless but when the palm trees that lined the driveway to a small pond came into view, we knew we were there.

Beside the pond was their cottage, nestled sweetly before lemon, banana and mango trees. This all gave the illusion of it being more on a Caribbean Island than Mexico. It was the most beautiful place I had ever seen in the five years of my life.

On the first night that we were there, I was allowed to sleep with my grandparents in their bedroom. It was riveting for me. I would be sleeping with the only two people who knew my mother when she was my age.

The furniture and curtains divided the bedrooms. My grandparent's bedroom was directly next to the kitchen and front entrance. In the centre of the kitchen was a wood burning stove that remained lit throughout the night.

It was my comforting blanket. It broke the sheet of darkness that engulfed the farm and cottage.

As we slept, the howls of a coyote crept through the silence. It was difficult for me to ignore the howling and fall back to asleep. When sleep had begun to take over again, my grandfather leapt out of the bed, grabbed his rifle, cocked it and ran out of the cottage, firing into the night. Within a few minutes the howling stopped and the only noise I could hear were from the crickets and frogs near the pond.

The next few days were filled with the hunting and the slaughtering of livestock. One day my grandfather told my mother that he had decided to take me with him on his horse and wagon. I was ecstatic about going with him. It was a new adventure, and one I would never forget.

He lifted me onto the wagon and loaded it with packages of freshly slaughtered meat. Once it was fully stocked, he struck his whip, making his horse gallop forward down the dirt road. The first village we visited set the pattern for what we would continue to see throughout the day.

In each village, children, almost naked and barefoot, with smoke funnelling around them kicked up by their feet, rushed towards the wagon with hands extended and begging for sweets and food. My grandfather would smile at them, motioning for them to get their parents or an elder.

The elder would appear, kiss my grandfather's hand and take the package from him. This went on for several hours and towards the end I fell asleep on the wagon not aware of the exact time of our return to the cottage.

I drowsily awoke to the whispers of voices and my grandfather's hands lifting me gently from the wagon onto his bed. I didn't want them to know I was awake.I pretended to sleep so I could wake up next to him in the morning.

The following morning I was awakened by a gruff voice scolding me for sleeping too long. It was time to work. I got dressed and went out with the field hands and helped them load packages onto the wagon again. They joked and laughed as they handed me more packages. It was obvious I wasn't really helping, but they wanted me to believe I was.

After they finished loading the wagon, my grandfather sat me down for a lecture. He wanted to talk to me about Cuba and Fidel Castro, and the wonderful work he was doing to unite Latin America. The days passed quickly, and it was time to return to Chicago. It was a tearful farewell. My mother cried during the whole journey back. It was the last time she saw her father alive.

When we returned to Chicago, my father took my mother into their bedroom. I knew something was wrong. He was nervous, restless and chain smoking. We'd later find out that on the second day of our visit in Mexico my father had been beaten up while working in the boiler room of the apartment unit. He made the mistake of retaliating, and was fearful they'd come after him again.

They did. Within less than a week of our return, my father was attacked at the front entrance of the apartment unit and stabbed seventeen times and left for dead.

At around that time, racial tension was mounting rapidly in the area. The attacks on the apartment unit became more frequent, forcing the tenants to flee. They advised my parents to do the same. Although my father was still recovering from the stabbings, he refused to go, making simple routines for us -like walking home from school - nearly impossible.

The summer of 1962 was the last summer my mother and siblings travelled to Wisconsin to work side by side in the fields. I spent it mostly alone playing with butterflies, rabbits and ladybugs. It was also the summer Marilyn Monroe died and the summer my father bought us a small portable black and white television. He performed the amazing feat of rigging cables and wires from nearby electrical lines into the abandoned shack we were staying in.

I can still recall the black and white news footage of the reports of Marilyn's death, her sheeted body lying on the gurney, and being loaded into the ambulance, as flash bulbs burst. The next moment they showed a short scene from when she sang "Happy birthday Mr. President." That summer was marked by Marilyn's death, but it was also the death of an era for my family.

When my mother returned to Chicago that summer, she gave my father an ultimatum. He either made plans to leave the west side or she would leave him. My father didn't argue.

He knew the years my mother had spent working on the fields were over. He told her we would move as soon as he found work.

In 1963, the local A&P Grocers on Madison Avenue was torched. There was shooting, looting and vandalism - and not a police car in sight. Unbelievably, my father sent my older brothers to retrieve what they could of the booty. My mother sobbed, begging them not to go out into the night. They returned an hour later with boxes of food and toys for their younger siblings

Several days later posters and flyers of Malcolm X appeared everywhere. Tension was increasing again. It was only a matter of time before it exploded into complete chaos.

One evening my father staggered in from a drinking spree, sat down at the table and began to cry. It was the first time I had ever seen him cry.

He told my mother, “I cannot win, woman. I cannot win. The whites hate me because they think I am Mexican. The Mexicans think I’m just a stupid Indian. The Negroes want to kill us! No matter who it is, I will never be good enough. I just can’t win!”

It was then that I realized we were different and we had no identity at all. Several months later, my dad found work in the north side community of Lakeview, at a thirty-six-unit apartment building.

He moved the family there; within a short time of our move, my mother discovered she was expecting her ninth child. And, within three years, she accomplished what she always set out to do. She purchased a home for her children.

Life steadily improved, but whether my parents ever finally found happiness in Chicago was always left up for debate.

MEMORIES OF CHILDHOOD

When I was quite young, I thought writing poetry would always be second nature to me, as everyone in my family thought too. I was always making up poems and singing songs. My parents; who enjoyed listening to my songs, encouraged me to recite and sing in front of their friends and relatives. But one day I found I couldn't recite anymore. My child spirit had flown away.

Everyone wondered how it could have happened. How could it have just disappeared in just one night? And, as the years passed, I tried many times to call it back, but it would never answer my calls. I wondered where it had gone. Where had I lost it? I tried to close my eyes to feel its presence but I felt nothing.

Finally, one day I thought I had found the answer. I travelled back in my mind to the summers when my mother and older siblings endured the hardships of working in the fields. Although those summers were a hardship for them; they held the fondest memories for me as a child. As I reminisced, I was five years old again.

I could smell the honeysuckle and strawberry fields nearby and envisioned myself sitting on the one step of the abandoned shack that my father had declared would be our summer home.

Next to the shack was the water pump that would provide water for bathing and cooking, and the cleverly covered electrical lines that my father had conveniently strung during the night from the main lines of the nearby houses so we could have electricity.

I'd remember his smile, his pat on my head to behave and his half wave before leaving for Chicago's west side's tenement building where he worked as a janitor and where we lived.

The remnants of the split shells of stolen watermelon from the neighbouring farm that we had eaten the night before lay uncovered in the makeshift bin and I'd remembered how I would awaken, jumping from bed ready to start the day playing and bouncing about with my dishevelled hair and bare feet.

I'd raise my hands to the sun and dance gleefully underneath it, and he, the sun, greeted me brightly as did the sparrows and the butterflies. I recalled the early morning start for the fields and remembered anxiously watching my mother board the old 1956 Chevy with my older brothers while I waited, anticipating their calling me to sit on their laps.

The butterflies sat neatly on my hair waiting for when there'd be no adults about to intrude on our play. The truck stopped and off everyone went into the fields to pick onions, potatoes, cucumbers, or whatever it was that needed picking—and off I went wandering about waiting for my friends to reappear and play with me again.

The ladybugs were the most accommodating. They would sit on my finger, transfixed until I would move them to my hair for all to admire and wonder if they were real. Skipping along I would recite under my breath to the sun, the butterflies and all who would ask for a poem.

"Recite to us dear child," the sun would say.

I would take a moment to ponder, and then I would begin,

'Pretty sun oh so sweet
I can feel you touch my feet
They get dirty every day
When I run and kick and play'

Then the butterflies would say while fluttering their wings,

"Recite to us dear child."

'Butterflies oh so nice
You are nicer than other flies
You are pretty with colours I like
And, you never make me want to fight'

Each time I recited the butterflies would sit on my nose or dance around my shoulders, opening and closing their wings. My child spirit was strong and it was easy to think of songs and poems to recite all day. Then one day, after reciting and singing new songs, it began to rain and I could hear my brothers calling out to me.

"Cookie, it's time to go. Come on, before it starts raining harder."

I ran to my brother who scooped me up into his arms and rubbed my arms to make sure I wasn't cold. He placed me on his lap while everyone huddled together to stay warm. But for me the rain was cool and wet and tickled me as it descended.

My mother took me into her arms and screeched that I smelled like a wet dog. Everyone started laughing, taking turns in ruffling my hair and hugging me. The truck made an abrupt stop at a rest area so my mother could clean me up.

There were other mothers with little girls who had blond hair and blue eyes, who wore pretty braids with ribbons and frilly dresses. I heard their mommy tell them not to get near me. Then, someone shouted, "Whites only. Get out!"

There was silence. No one said anything. That night, after my bath, I lay still in my bed. I thought about the little girls with the pretty ribbons and the mommy who wouldn't let me use the toilet at the rest area. I called my child spirit to sing with me to help me feel better but instead....it said, "Goodbye!"

Days would pass where I would call my child spirit back, but it would never come. One day I stopped calling.

Many years later, in a dark room in Southampton, England, my child spirit flew back and sang to me. It helped me reach down, take pen and paper into my hand and write poems again -and afterwards I sang the chant of my ancestors to my child spirit, so that it may never go away again.

A RACE IN FLIGHT

"Come on, hurry up! What do you want to drink? Let's go to the corner restaurant and have a coke? Damn niggers! They're everywhere!"

I cringed when he said "niggers". I hated that word. I couldn't understand why he had to use it all the time when we were together. I am not white. Each time he said it; it reminded me how much I wasn't.

Randy was six feet tall and burly for seventeen. He was older than me, by four years. But it felt like he was twenty years older by his sometimes serious tone. His raspy voice, clear blue eyes and rough features made him an ideal candidate for Hollywood. I swooned when I first saw him, but he made me flinch when he started talking about how much he hated foreigners and blacks.

His first words to me when we were introduced at a party were, "What country are you from, lil bit?" I explained no country, just this one. He hugged me, which startled me. Then he said "I always wanted me an Indian girl!"

Later that evening he told me he was part Chickasaw. I chuckled inside at the thought. Now that was a blood line that hadn't been claimed before. It had begun to appear to me that every white person I would meet had some Indian blood in them.

They were always either half or a quarter of something Indian; Cherokee, Apache, Sioux, it always made me wonder how on earth any Indians wound up on the reservations at all, and how, if they were part Indian, could they ever be racist?

But there was a strong possibility he was. He didn't have the pale colouring that most white people had. His black hair made him resemble an Italian from the Mediterranean shores, not those of the Mississippi river.

My dark olive skin, hair and eyes fascinated Randy as well. He would intertwine our fingers and compare our skin colour. It wasn't long before our days together turned into weeks and then months. We spent almost every day talking, walking and sometimes sitting for hours in Montrose Park under his favourite tree. We'd look out at the lake and sit together like young lovers. Many times, as he shifted his body close to mine, I'd lay my head on his lap, and he'd stroke my face while recalling his childhood trips with his father to the Appalachian Mountains.

I loved the stories of his childhood, the fishing trips with his father, frying their catch along the river, his enthusiasm when he'd recall the smells of the Mississippi Pine and the grandeur of the Elm. It was poetry when he'd repeat the bed time stories his mother told him about the magic of the Cottonwood tree whose flowers can be spun into cotton for the finest suits and dresses. I could visualise it all with each pause and long Mississippi drawl.

There was innocence when he reminisced, and a sadness of leaving his home for a city that he obviously didn't like. He would talk about his mother, her struggles, and the small town in Mississippi where she was from, and where she met Randy's father.

"There was no work in Mississippi. Not enough to live on or eat," he'd say despondently. "He wanted to start a new life in West Virginia, so we moved there. The next year, he died in a mining accident." Randy recalled as his voice faded to a murmur. He would leave me for his memories while I waited for him to come back to me.

Life changed for Randy and his mother after his father died. His mother, an illiterate, kindly small-framed woman, didn't understand or know what to do after the death of her husband. So she did the only thing she could do. She moved back to her home town in Mississippi, taking Randy, who was just a little boy, with her.

Leaving West Virginia was a dull and painful memory. Randy's mother took work where she could find it. After a couple of months of washing clothing for black maids of wealthy landowners, a friend of Randy's mother suggested they move to Chicago.

Within a month of leaving Mississippi for Chicago's Uptown area, she found a job as a seamstress in a drycleaner. Several years earlier there had been an exodus of poor white Southerners to Chicago, and because of the numbers resettling there, it was quickly nicknamed "Hillbilly Heaven." It quickly became home for Randy and his mother.

Hillbilly Heaven had become a haven for many White Southerners. They understood and helped each other with information on work, city services, housing and food. The housing conditions were horrific though. Many of the houses were plagued with rotting walls, roaches and rodents. Living under those conditions, it was hard to make it under any standards.

There was state aid for poor families called ADC, a financial aid program available for families with small children. It was a relief package for many in Uptown who met the criteria for assistance but Randy's mother didn't. "And anyway," he would say, "she prefers to work."

Her sacrifice and the guilt he felt because of it made it difficult for Randy to focus on school. He preferred to quit and work full time, and he'd talk about us getting married too. But I didn't want to. I told him I was too young. I was only thirteen.

I think many times I was his escape from the realities of his life. A life that he probably felt was dealt to him unfairly. He was sentenced to live within a city that he couldn't relate to or understand.

He hated that he was treated as poor white trash by other whites in Chicago, with their opinions and treatment solely based on his southern accent. I understood his pain, and he relished in the fact that I did.

"I love you, little Cinnamon," he said often to me while lovingly lifting my hundred pounds, five-foot two-inch frame, which fit perfectly in his arms, and cradling me like a baby.

He'd kiss me several times before leaving me at the door of my parents' home and wait until I was safely inside. And then he would be back at my front door in the morning waiting to spend the day with me.

But today was different: He was moody and impatient and it didn't look like he was going to make any proclamations of love to me, or want to spend an entire day with me either.

"What do ya want to drink? Can't ya hear?" I was shocked and frightened by his tone. I became more nervous with each quickened step as I struggled to keep up. Walking towards the restaurant, we passed Wilson Park where three black children, about eight or nine years old, were playing baseball. The sight of them in the park made Randy fume.

"Hey, you, fuckin' niggers! Get out of our neighbourhood before I kill you!" he said with venomous hatred that spewed from his lips. I stared in horror hardly able to recognise the boy who had just carried me in his arms the night before.

"Randy, they're only playing, they're just kids!"

"Shut up! Don't you tell me what I can say to a buncha niggers!"

I moved quickly towards the restaurant, hoping Randy would follow. To my relief he did, although he continued to turn and stare threateningly at the boys in the park.

Near the restaurant's entrance, a woman holding a child in her lap, sat on the concrete sidewalk. She stretched out her hand and begged for money. Randy, livid, practically spat at her.

He pulled hard at the restaurant door, stormed in, found a booth and waited for me to sit next to him. I hesitated, finally sliding in by his side.

"Can't you see what's wrong with those people? They don't wanna work! They want everything easy!

Look at my ma who worked all her life. She don't sit out there asking for money!"

I didn't dare say a word. Randy's unfamiliar solemn expression, to my relief, softened to a gentler one and his childish grin returned. He was my Randy again, but the calm didn't last. The booth overlooked the park we had just passed, and the children who had been playing baseball were still there.

We ordered a Coke and said nothing until our drinks arrived.

While we drank the cold drink, Randy kept looking over to the park. His previous grimace returned in a flash.

"Fuckin' niggers! Look they're still there!"

I am not sure why I stayed quiet. It might have been due to the anxiety and panic I was feeling at the time. Without a second's warning, Randy threw money on the table and rushed out of the restaurant. I followed close behind as he marched up to the boys who were playing baseball.

The boy who was up to bat froze and stared at Randy. You could see he was terrified of him. I couldn't believe what happened next.

Without any provocation from the children, Randy punched the young batter in the face knocking him over. And, within seconds, out of nowhere, several of Randy's friends ran over and began shouting for him to hit him again. The other little black boys who had been playing baseball began to scatter and run out of the park; leaving their friend at the mercy of his attackers.

I was in shock. I started to say something but before I could, Randy picked up the baseball bat, swung the bat around, and struck the little boy across the face. There were woops of laughter from the people in the park and his friends squealed with joy, egging him on again. I screamed in horror for him to stop and grabbed at his arm to hold him back.

"Stop, Randy, please…he is only a little boy!" I cried. Randy, without thinking, slapped me violently which caused me to stagger and fall next to the boy. He flinched, showing me that it was more involuntary than deliberate, but he quickly caught himself.

Sitting next to the little boy I could hear him breathing heavily with fear. I looked at Randy who was staring down at him with contempt and hatred. His stares made my blood go cold which made me panic more. Thinking he might strike the little boy again, I turned my body over him, forming a bridge to protect him.

"Move Cinnamon, move or I'll kill you too!"

"Kill me then!" I shrieked, my eyes flooding with

tears I moved to the side and held the boy's face, which was covered in blood, in my hand. There was a painful expression in Randy's eyes before they welled with tears. He was staring at me helplessly, searching for sympathy. His voice rang out again.

"Cinnamon, move, move..."

"Kill me, because I am not moving!" Floods of tears streamed down my cheeks.

"Fuck you. You nigger lover! You better be careful. You are this close to being a nigger yourself!" Randy held his index finger and thumb close together leaving a fragment of a gap to show how close I was to being black.

I could hear police sirens chiming from a distance, growing louder and louder until they became a roaring sound. A friend of Randy's pulled his arm urgently to signal him to run and within seconds the park was almost empty. Randy stood there, staring at me and the little boy. He moved closer toward me, extending his hand to help me to my feet.

I turned towards the little boy instead, pulling him closer to me. I sobbed as I stared into his eyes. They were dilated and his little body lay limp in my arms. His shirt, soaked in blood, stained mine as I held onto him protectively.

Randy watched me hold the little boy. There was sadness in his eyes, a sadness I had become familiar with when he'd talk about his father. His face softened and his voice pleading. He stretched out his hand again to help me up.

"Please. Let's go!" he wailed with his head lowered. He made a final gesture for me to leave with him. I shook my head, pulling the boy tighter towards my chest. Tears flowed down Randy's cheeks. We both knew we would never see each other again. The distant voices became louder and the sirens blared nonstop. Randy turned and ran away.

THE COLA POEM

Sitting in a diner parched for a drink
Nothing will do—but a cool, cool cola in the late afternoon
I sip the dark liquid as it glides down my throat
And relish the sweet syrup as if it were gold
Nothin' matters, nothin' at all
Who cares about the screams from the woman afar
She's been mugged by an addict
Who has no money for a fix
She cries for pity but there's none to give

He leaves her alone—while she sobs her last breath

Sitting in a diner parched for a drink
Nothing will do—but a cool, cool cola in the late afternoon
I sip the dark liquid as it glides down my throat
And relish the sweet syrup as if it were gold
Nothin' matters, nothin' at all...

In the distance
A small black child cries
He's been playing ball at the park nearby
He's been beaten—

FEEDING MY CHILDREN

His head smashed in
His eyes are blackened
His nose sunken—from the fist that struck him
He should have known better
That park was for people of the right colour

Sitting in a diner parched for a drink
Nothing will do but a cool, cool cola in the late afternoon
I sip the dark liquid as it glides down my throat
And relish the sweet syrup as if it were gold
Nothin' matters, nothin' at all

A woman sits outside the door on the concrete street
Begging for money and something to eat
No one sees her—they just try to avoid
If you give her money she'll just want more

Sitting in a diner parched for a drink
Nothing will do but a cool, cool cola in the late afternoon
I sip the dark liquid as it glides down my throat
And relish the sweet syrup as if it were gold
Nothin' matters, nothin' at all.

NAVAJO

It was late, and I had been standing for over half an hour in the queue trying to buy my ticket for Arizona. When it was finally my turn, I handed over my credit card and asked for the midnight bus to Flagstaff.

The woman at the desk ran my credit card and circled gate eleven in red on my ticket. She was about to hand it to me, but instead she turned to look at the clock that hung over the exit, and said the bus I was about to take frequently gets cancelled because they couldn't justify the route at that time slot. She then handed me my ticket and said, "Good Luck."

I smiled nervously at her and said under my breath that I hoped there wouldn't be any delays or cancellations. Walking with my ticket in my hand, I scanned the opened doors with numbers on top and presumed they were the gate numbers. My eyes finally settled on a door that read "Eleven" and with a sigh of relief I walked towards it.

There were several people with luggage, blankets, pillows, bags and food lined up in front of the gate. I thought it would be wise to do the same.

The man at the end of the line wore a cowboy hat, boots and well worn jeans and just as I settled behind him he turned, smiled and reassuringly gestured for me to stand in front of him. I declined.

His silent welcome helped me relax about the possibility of no bus, and I pulled off my backpack and laid it close by me. I like cowboys, I thought to myself. They are always so polite.

The cowboy turned around again, looked at me, tipped his hat and smiled, "Hallo, little darlin'," he said.

I sighed and returned his smile with mine. Yes, sir, I thought, he was a cowboy by all descriptions of the name. Just as soon as I flopped down on the floor about twenty people lined up behind me, with their luggage, bags of food, pillows and blankets. I slid my derriere closer to the cowboy's leather boot heels as he turned around and chuckled.

Holding my pack tightly against my chest, I let my eyes scan the station walls, finally settling them on the clock that read eleven fifteen. How could so many people be taking a bus that might not come, and at that time of night? Don't they have a life?' They all couldn't possibly be going to Flagstaff?

When I called the Greyhound station for the times of departure I was told to be an hour early. What an idiot, I thought. I wasn't catching a flight where I had to go through security clearance like the airports. And then it dawned on me that she might have said to come early so I would be sure to secure a seat. But so far, from what I could see, it looked safe as far as getting a seat on the bus.

"What am I? Number eleven or twelve in line waiting?" I said out loud, not caring if anyone thought I was a nut. I looked around again and couldn't believe how old the station looked.

The walls were dingy grey, seats broken and the tiled floors were faded and worn. This was Las Vegas, fifteen minutes from the strip. We were in the United States, not a third world country.

I also started to wonder how many people left Vegas via bus with just the shirt on their backs. But, the people in the station didn't look like gamblers. They were Mexican migrant farm workers, cowboys, poor whites and blacks, probably all erroneously thinking it was cheaper to take a bus rather than purchasing an airplane ticket. Poor saps!

Wait a minute. I thought, I was one of those saps. What was I thinking? Weirder still, some of the people who were standing and waiting in the station looked like the same people I saw the last time I rode a bus. When was that? Nearly fifteen years ago.

After that journey I swore I would never take another bus again. I spent it with drunken couples, children with lice jumping from their heads, and getting robbed of my camera and coin purse while I was sleeping. Was I in a time warp?

Get a grip, I told myself. This wasn't the Twilight Zone. The bus ride was only a five-hour drive, if that.

Ted would meet me at the station. We'd have breakfast and then drive to the reservation.

The thought of meeting Ted made my heart beat faster and my palms sweat. I didn't know what to expect, let alone what to do on an Indian reservation. What would it be like?

I felt a moment of dread and remembered my dad. I wished I could see him again so I could speak to him about our history, culture and ancestors.

I grew up accepting our customs and routines as normal, finding other cultures and ethnicities more intriguing than ours. But, as time passed I made a discovery, although to some obvious, that our culture was just as intriguing as any other. It was an obvious truth that kept jumping out at me whenever someone asked me where my parents were from.

The only problem with my cultural epiphany was, I didn't know where start to understand it better? My father had always identified as being Indian. There was no argument there, but he never elaborated further. He never shared his thoughts on how it compared to other cultures or why ours was different. Nor did he explain to us where our family fell in the larger picture of Native American groups. I wanted to know. I needed to know.

I am sure if I asked him today, he would say to me "who cares?" but for some reason…I cared.

Maybe it was the whole sharing of community stuff. I hoped meeting Ted would help me get a better handle and perspective on things.

MASSACRE ON THE RESERVATION

Listen, can you hear?
There are voices speaking but no one there
They call out in the night
Pleading...for justice
For their lives have been stolen
Without a fight

They bled along the unpaved street
While they stumbled
Dragging their injured feet

They raised their arms in defeat
Praying for redemption
And their lives to keep

Their pleas were futile—supplications scorned
Mocked and discarded—
Poor injured souls.

NAVAJO

During my last telephone conversation with Ted, while trying to smooth out the last details of where and when we would meet, his tone became increasingly haughty and condescending, with particularly heavy reference to him being a full-blooded Navajo.

What was he implying? I was mixed and he wasn't? His calculated references to race made me wince, and before I could say goodbye and see you soon, he slammed the phone down. I was certain that his manner in hanging up the phone was not deliberate but he made me feel uncomfortable and apprehensive about going to meet him.

Ted was a fluke meeting via the internet. I was researching my ancestral background when I came across one of his articles on the Navajo. After several emails and telephone exchanges we decided it was time to meet and talk.

I had been looking forward to this day but I wasn't so sure now. If the last phone call was any indication of what he was really like, what would it be like staying with him for a few days?

The whispers of the other passengers, saying the bus scheduled to depart at midnight might not be leaving after all, replaced my fear of meeting Ted with whether I would be able to contact him to tell him that I might not be arriving after all.

It was five minutes to midnight, and it all looked very grim, when someone said they thought they saw a bus nearing the bay. The people who were at the top of the line, and nearest to the gate, were not going to take any chances on a stampede.

They stood up, with their pillows shoved under their arms, and their suitcases close to their feet, and began pushing their suitcases up to the gate for quick boarding. They waited with bated breath, but it was a false alarm. Our bus hadn't come, but it didn't matter.

The once-pessimistic travellers lined up behind each other in orderly fashion. I decided it might be wise for me to get back up to my feet. I wrapped the straps of my backpack around my shoulders and stood neatly behind the cowboy.

"Where you going little lady?" he said with a familiar southern flair.

"Flagstaff. Where are you going?"

"Phoenix, darlin'. I live just outside there in a little town nobody ever heard of. Ya got family in Flagstaff?"

"No. Not really, just visiting a friend."

"Well, it looks like you're in luck cus there's the

bus." I smiled and prepared to make my dash for the bus to secure my seat.

"Better check the time on your watch cus I think there's a time difference." The cowboy tipped his hat, handed his bus ticket to the driver and boarded the bus. He found a seat at the rear while I chose to sit towards the front. I was relieved. I had said a quick prayer earlier that no one would sit next to me, and to my surprise, no-one did.

I settled into my seat, knees up against the seat in front of me, arms tucked under each other and head leaning against the window. I was ready to sleep and started to drift off, when I recalled my last experience on a Greyhound bus. Alarm bells began ringing in my head. Maybe falling asleep on the bus might not be a good idea. I didn't want to get robbed again. I regretted my desire not to have anyone sit next to me—they would have kept me awake. It was too late now, I had to stay awake, but within minutes of our departure, I fell asleep.

I woke up with a sudden jolt to find the bus turning into the Flagstaff station. Amazed that I had slept through the entire journey and grateful that I didn't miss my stop, I strained my eyes through the bus window to see if Ted was where he had promised to be. He wasn't.

Instead, where he had promised he would be

waiting, stood a few vagrants begging near the entrance. Disappointed, I rubbed my eyes, grabbed my backpack along with the other passengers who were quickly pulling their bags off the overhead racks, and wandered alongside them into an empty bus station. Not sure what to do next I sat down on one of the brown wooden benches...and waited.

After fifteen minutes of waiting, I began to feel foolish and decided to wait outside. Where was Ted? I took a deep breath, looked around and noticed a deeply tanned, moustached man with a long black pony tail peering at me from behind the corner of the bus station. He was studying me and probably had been watching me the entire time. It then registered to me that it was Ted. He smirked, acknowledging my realisation and walked towards me. Annoyed with him, I felt my face turn hot and red.

"Hungry?" he said dryly. "Let's get a bite to eat and we'll talk about the itinerary for the day. My truck is parked at the back of the station. Come on."

Ted patted my backpack, pulled it away from me and led the way. We were about to pull out of the parking lot, when one of the two vagrants who had been standing in front of the bus station entrance pushed his hand into Ted's window and began begging in Navajo.

"Sorry pal," Ted said. "I don't speak Navajo." I smirked and thought. Full bloodied Navajo and he doesn't speak the language, doesn't say much about keeping up with tradition.

"I am a Navajo brother. Do ya got any change?" the vagrant said, repeating his plea in English. He struggled with his balance while his friend stood by nodding. His face, darkened by the sun and ruddy from too much drinking, was difficult to look at. Ted frowned, searched through his pockets, handed him a few coins, put the truck into gear, floored his foot on the accelerator and roared out of the parking lot leaving a trail of smoke behind him.

I held on to my seat while Ted continued to gun the motor to get as far as he could from the bus station. I could see he was embarrassed and frustrated by the vagrant.

He drove with his eyes fixed on the road and in awkward silence. It was that awkward silence that is a little too quiet for comfort and you think maybe you should say something to break the ice, but it would probably be better not.

We drove for a quarter of an hour, until practically every building we passed looked the same to me. I stared blankly out of the truck window thinking of my father and uncles who were all alcoholics. Any of them could have easily been one of those vagrants at the station. I remembered my uncle, whom I felt Ted bore an uncanny resemblance to, disappearing regularly and appearing on the street corner on what was once known as Chicago's "skid row," begging and in a near drunken coma. My father and his other brothers would eventually find him and take him home to recover.

I never understood why they did this to themselves or to their families. For the longest time I was ashamed to identify myself with anything Indian. Now I was sitting next to someone who epitomized everything that was Native.

HOW I MISS THAT LIFE

How I miss that life
A life so divine
Of bare feet, tousled hair, playing wildly in the street
Mother calling, 'It's late—get in—time to eat!'
Eight more children come a-running – ready for her to feed
Tortillas on the table, sweet corn and breaded beef
Father sitting on his chair, barely able to speak
Drunk, from drinking beer only minutes before
Which he purchased earlier, from the corner store
No one takes any notice, or utters a word

Without warning, a thud is heard
Children scatter, searching for a fallen coin
Then father is left, where he fell
Snoring, till the morning.

NAVAJO

I studied Ted's features with curious fascination. I had never found anything attractive about any of the men in my family and couldn't understand what my mother saw in my father. But staring at Ted, I realised there was strength in each line and curve of his face.

I wish I could have noticed years before my father died the beauty of his features. I felt sad and lonely and found myself so deep in thought that when Ted tried to say something, I barely heard him.

"We're here, wake up!" We walked into a Denny's type diner and were seated by a friendly robust blond waitress whose smile appeared to be contagious. I smiled back effortlessly and then looked to see if all the patrons in the restaurant were smiling too as they ate; they were.

Were they smiling because Ted and I walked in together? Two Natives ready to talk important Native issues. Did I look different? Did they even know I was Native too, true to the saying "birds of a feather flock together?"

We settled into our booth and Ted instantly started to explain that he had never lived anywhere else but the reservation. I listened intently and at the same time in awe, never interrupting. It was obvious to him that I admired him. I hung on to hear every word. He was amazingly articulate and well spoken.

Then a wave of guilt came over me. How terrible of me to think that he wouldn't be.

Why shouldn't he be articulate? It then crossed my mind why I thought he might not be. He still lived in the reservation and worked as a labourer. It dawned on me that I had become a product of my environment, a true Chicago snob.

I had turned into one of those people I had criticised for years. People who preferred to measure everyone by their academic and professional accomplishments rather than their character and social morals.

Who did I think I was? I may have grown up in an affluent area, but it didn't start out that way. The first eight years of my life were spent in dire poverty, and my educational background was nothing to shout about either. If my mother hadn't had the common sense to invest in land, we would all still be working in the fields as field hands.

While I was chastising myself for being the loathsome creature that I had become, Ted rattled on about the loss of his wife and the book they had written together. He had no clue of the internal battle I had just won. Relieved it was over I listened with even more conviction. It was then that I realized that Ted was a back seat writer.

He wrote the book, wrote the perspectives, got it published and then took a back seat to it, giving all credit to his deceased wife. I could see his frustration as he talked, and I understood why he chose that course of action. If his book got ridiculed or rejected, he was in the back seat. No one would know he was the actual driver. No harm, no foul. It was a coward's way out.

How foolish, I thought. I wondered if Ted realised that I could see right through him?

There was another thing that I noticed about him as he continued to talk. Each time I tried to ask a question; he would not let me. After an hour of not being allowed to exchange views, I came to realize he had a quality (or fault) I didn't like: he was egotistical. So much so that it was irritating. He had mentioned that many people in the reservation didn't like him. I could see why. I found myself withdrawing to a quieter more observant character.

"Are you ready to leave?" Ted said, grabbing the check and making his way to pay. He strutted and grinned flirtatiously at the waitresses. I sat and watched him closely as he paid the bill. It was true, he resembled my uncle and it made me uncomfortable. But there was an air of confidence that my uncle lacked.

I took a deep breath, pushing my childhood

memories of my uncle to the side. I didn't want my bad thoughts of him to interfere with my interaction with Ted. I wanted to feel relaxed around him, so I observed him more intensely.

His dark tan and muscular build made him look younger than his fifty years. Also, his long black hair showed little to no grey and his face although rugged had little to no facial lines or wrinkles. I wouldn't say he was an attractive man, at least not by my standards, but I could see how other women might find him so.

I waited for him to come back to our table. When he walked out of the restaurant without saying a word, I awkwardly searched through my bag for a few dollars to leave for a tip, gathered all my stuff, and ran out.

I found Ted sitting behind the wheel waiting, stroking his moustache and smirking. His arrogance and ego unnerved me. At that moment I couldn't decide who he reminded me more of, my uncle or Ali, a Muslim Iranian boyfriend, who always made me trail behind him whenever we went out.

"What do you want to do this morning?" he said, staring blankly forward. "Hurry up and decide. We are in Flagstaff and it's a three-hour drive to Chinle," he continued.

I was content that he'd finally brought up an itinerary, as I had a suggestion. "Is Flagstaff close to

Sedona?" Ted, surprised by my question, turned his head towards me and tightened his hands on the steering wheel in amazement.

"Sedona? Why do you want to go to Sedona?" I shrugged my shoulders and didn't reply. He turned the ignition switch and began to drive, not giving any hint of a destination or whether he had considered my request at all. Not sure what to say next, I continued to look out the window until he pulled into a motel car park.

"I am tired. I need a nap. This morning started out way too early, any objections?" I didn't know what to say.

I watched him get out of the truck and walk into the motel reception office. I wondered whether I should demand to be taken back to the bus station or just wait and see what was really on his mind.

Giving him the benefit of the doubt, I thought, maybe he was tired and all he really wanted to do was sleep.

Anyway, what was the big deal? I wasn't a teenager anymore, trying to hold onto my virtue. That was long gone. But, being at a motel, with a man I barely knew, did bother me.

Ted walked out of the motel reception office and past the pick-up truck to a room a few doors down from where we were parked. Holding a key in his hand he opened the door and went inside without so much as a wave or a look.

I was surprised that he had ignored me, or asked me whether I was okay with the idea of staying in a motel. I walked slowly out of the truck to the room and found him lying on one of two single beds, naked, face down on the pillow.

I wasn't sure how to react or whether I should be appreciative that he asked for a double room. He didn't say a word to me. I stood at the door, waiting, not knowing whether to lie down or walk out while he slept. The silence was quickly interrupted by his muffled words.

"Are you attracted to me? I am not to you, so go to sleep." I was embarrassed and clumsily climbed into the other bed and decided I would try to go to sleep. Within a few minutes, Ted crept over into my bed.

His naked body pressed against mine, and his hot breath made it almost impossible for me to breathe. "It's only sex—just sex—that's all I want," he said.

I took a deep breath, closed my eyes and remembered Frankie. She said, 'Go to Sedona. The person who takes you will ask to bed you, do not feel ashamed. It must be, so you can get the answers you need.'

He placed his hand on my bottom and then moved it along to the front of my jeans and undid the clasp. I took another deep breath. At first, intimidated by his strength and stunned by his assertiveness; I gave in, taking comfort in Frankie's words but too paralysed to make any movement at all.

A few hours had passed when I awoke with a jolt. I couldn't believe I had fallen asleep. I could hear the shower going and jumped up to look at my watch. It was only thirty minutes before noon. We still had the entire day ahead of us.

I awkwardly walked into the bathroom while he was walking out. I lowered my head too embarrassed to look at him, not really understanding why I was reacting the way I was. I quickly washed, redressed and was out the door.

Ted was standing next to his truck, patiently waiting and holding the door open for me. I slid into the passenger side, still too embarrassed to look him in the eye.

"I asked you earlier what you wanted to do. Still want to go to Sedona?" He said flinging his head back and loosening his hair from the band that held it together. The raven strands spilled over his shoulders and glistened against his dark skin.

"Yes, well.... I don't know. An elderly friend of mine, who was from Arizona, spoke about it all the time. She said that Sedona was a magical place. I want to see if it's true, but if you don't want to go...I mean...I won't mind." Ted grinned.

"Well, it's a pretty place and all, but I don't know about it being magical. I took my wife there once. Maybe it's time to go again. Let's go."

"Is it far?" It was a stupid question. I should have asked that question before asking whether he could take me there.

"Naw, it's about an hour drive but it will take us a little longer to get to Chinle. I'll call my kids to let them know I will be getting there later. They can get their dinner together themselves. They are pretty independent."

"I am taking you away from your kids." I said, swallowing hard and letting guilt sink in.

"Don't sweat it. I get home late all the time when I'm doing business."

I didn't want to think of the motel episode again, but he was already acting as if we had just met. I thought it better to act as if nothing had happened too. I would stick to what we had agreed and concentrate only on talking about life in the reservation, Indian ways, and the progress of his book. There were also things I wanted to talk about, things I wanted to share. I needed and wanted him to be the right person to whom I could ask all my questions. I needed resolution.

Ted drove quietly, his eyes steadily set on the road. He appeared familiar and comfortable with the highway, but why wouldn't he be familiar? We drove for about forty-five minutes, first staring at nothing but boring, brown arid sand.

I couldn't understand why my friend thought this part of the country was so spectacular, but after a while, almost magically, the topography started to change.

First the trees began to multiply, merging almost together. Then the grass began to spread out, covering large stretches of land. The truck had also begun to ascend as the road narrowed and wound upwards, revealing the twists and turns of new landscapes of red, orange and yellow canyons.

As we continued to climb, the canyons peaked, becoming natural architectural wonders that resembled sculptures of men and women with Native American faces. It was all so unbelievable. I stared in amazement at how quickly it all changed.

After thirty minutes of colourful mountain views, the main town and high street came into sight.

Ted pulled up to a restaurant that resembled a 1950's New York diner, pulled into the car park, got out and walked in, leaving me behind. His lack of courtesy was becoming normal to me. But entering the diner was even more bizarre. It wasn't the type of diner I expected to find on top of a mountain in Arizona. I found Ted seated in a booth, staring blankly at an empty seat.

"The last time I was here I was with my wife. We sat over there." He pointed to the outside tables and then looked down at the menu quietly. His eyes watered while trying to read the menu. When the waiter appeared, I thought he was going to start to cry, but he didn't. We placed our orders and Ted fell silent again. I wanted to say something but I couldn't. To anyone, it might have appeared he was still mourning the death of his wife, but I couldn't help but feel his moment of emotion was staged.

He didn't speak or look at me while we waited for our food. Instead he became fidgety and anxious and there was no sign that he would be relaxing soon. I thought the silence would break when they brought our drinks but it didn't. We ate and drank in complete silence until just as we had almost finished our food.

"Well, what do you think of Sedona?" Ted said, staring impatiently, almost demanding.

"Oh, I'm sorry, I sort of drifted there. I think it's really beautiful! Great place really. Thank you so much for bringing me here, really."

Ted studied my face and then laughed. "Ah ha, you *really* like it." He said grinning widely. He eyed me carefully, and for the first time I felt he had become human, it was a welcome relief from his cold and distant attitude which intimidated me.

"Soooo, you do like it?" Ted said playfully again as he leaned closer to me, placing his elbows on the table and making me shrink just a bit.

I didn't want to tell him I was disappointed, especially after all the trouble he had gone through in driving me there. I thought of the canyons, their contrast of colours and how dramatically they'd change within each mile.

Although the changes were pretty, I felt it had all been overshadowed by the overpriced houses and gated communities; in my opinion, Sedona was an over rated town built up by realtors that wanted to get as high a percentage of sales as they could. But, maybe I was being harsh. Maybe…it lost what it once had. I took a deep breath and tried to feel the magic everyone had spoken of; I felt nothing. It was just another place, another tourist spot where people filled their shopping bags with trinkets and pottery that would eventually be sold in some garage sale or donated at a local charity shop.

Looking across the road from the restaurant my feelings were confirmed as I watched tourists pop in and out of ice-cream and coffee shops in their Bermuda shorts, funny-looking glasses and hats.

They would stop occasionally to gawk at a Native American Indian souvenir shop, not go in, and move on to the next one and gawk some more. I sighed in affirmation when my thoughts were interrupted by the tapping sounds of Ted's finger against his water glass. He stared insistently at me, waiting for my reply.

"Yes, I like it a lot. It's a great place, really." I said, as convincingly as possible.

"Who are you trying to convince, me or you? We better get going." Before I could offer to pay, Ted motioned the waiter over, paid the bill, and as before, walked out without waiting for me. I felt beaten again.

He walked back to the parking lot, looking taller and more confident. Grabbing at his pony-tail, and pulling off the band that held his hair together, he let his hair flow past his shoulders. Then tucked his hands underneath it, flicked it in an outward motion while he jerked his head like a peacock.

I sped up, all the time feeling like the caddy for the over-pompous golfer. I had now gone past annoyed. I was humiliated. Was he laughing at me? I wondered if he was. I was beginning to feel he was.

We had gone back to the same old brown boring desert of few homes and flat cliffs, and a drive done in silence until, after two hours, Ted cleared his throat. He turned and pointed out a few things to me and began to narrate what was unfolding before us. I wasn't listening. All I could hear was blah, blah, blah and then a murmur of something turned into something comprehensible.

"All of this is Navajo. There's about 250,000 square miles of federally allocated land which is mostly occupied by the Navajo Indian. This land extends from the north east corner of Arizona, New Mexico and Utah."

I looked around as Ted pointed into a barren desert. It then hit me. We had been driving across the reservation. I was IN the reservation, and it was massive. I never thought it would be this huge. But, what struck me most was how sparsely populated it was. Ted stopped his narrative and fell back into his mood of silence.

I watched the sun creep behind the clouds and canyons, hoping the desert would shift from its tawny colour and endless flat land. The hope of a change of topography dwindled as the sky grew greyer and the scenery disappeared into an empty haze.

I started to fall asleep when I felt the truck change direction and go off the paved road onto a dirt one. The pick-up bounced up and down, leaving a trail of dust behind it. I sat up to see where we were, but couldn't make anything out.

We continued to drive, nearly reaching the end of the road when I saw a dimly-lit trailer home ahead, with a makeshift extension propped on top of cement blocks. A dog began barking as we turned into the direction of the sounds.

Ted pulled up behind the trailer, parked and walked towards its entrance. That's when I noticed the house. It stood directly next to the trailer, a dilapidated affair that resembled more a shack than a house.

If that thing provided shelter for anything living it would be just barely. Creeping out of one of the windows, a glimmer of light caught my eye. Could there be people actually living in there?

Not too far from the house was a shed that was held together by planks of wood. A scraggily dog that looked as abandoned as the shed, jetted from underneath one of the planks and ran across the unpaved path to his owner, who violently kicked him to the side. The dog yelped in pain, dragged his tail between his legs, and cowered back underneath the planks.

There was nothing to suggest a garden or any type of homely warmth outside of a fence of old inner tubes, punctured tires and abandoned cars that stood next to each other, surrounding several cactus and rocks. The entire scene was painted grey…empty, lonely and eerie. Yet, strangely enough, exempt of the cold host and exterior, I was reminded of the early morning arrivals to the homes of our relatives in Texas.

I remembered the long eighteen-hour drive along Highway 55, then across Highway 10, when my parents took us to visit our relatives. Just as we'd arrive we would smell the flat bread and the woodburning from the old wooden stove.

The funnels of smoke hailed us for making our journey. Waiting relatives would rush to greet us, laughing as they'd shoo their rambunctious dogs to the side, while hurrying to take our luggage in. The younger cousins would storm out of the thin meshed doors, greeting us in their bare feet.

They'd chime in together, asking whether our journey was a good one. But this was not Texas, and there was no one running out to meet us, let alone greet us.

Ted walked into the trailer, slammed the door shut before I could walk in behind him. I stood there and waited for what felt like hours but was just thirty minutes at which time Ted popped up at the door.

"Come on in! What are you doing standing out there?" Ted turned around and walked back into the trailer.

I wasn't sure why, but I had actually thought he would be going into the house, not the trailer. I looked back towards the window where I had seen the glimmer of light. It was still there. There had to be people inside. Why didn't he go anywhere near it?

Walking into the trailer, I saw sitting on the floor in front of a television, a little boy with thick straight black hair and large round brown eyes.

He was about eight or nine years of age. I had barely said hello, when another boy about fourteen or fifteen years old, who looked strikingly similar to the smaller boy, walked in behind me. I turned to the right of me to discover that the living room was also the kitchen and dining room.

The boy didn't smile or make any gesture of greeting, but walked straight to his father, whispered something and left. The smaller boy did smile with an amused twinkle in his eye which almost compelled me to speak to him, but I didn't dare to.

"Okay son, it's time to go to bed!" Ted scolded the boy as he jumped to his feet from the floor and ran out of the trailer. He then turned and looked at me with a dismal expression.

"The sofa turns into a bed and you will be comfortable there. I've slept there a few times so it's not a bad sleep. The bathroom is in the house, and that's where the kids sleep too. The door is never locked so just walk in, turn to the right and you will see the bathroom ahead.I just did the laundry so there are clean towels. You should be able to find them without a problem. Good night. I'll see you in the morning."

Ted walked past me into a bedroom that was at the foot of the room and closed the door. I was left alone. I sighed with relief at not having to talk to him anymore, but at the same time
I felt…abandoned.

I sat staring at the door we had walked through just a few minutes earlier. I was numb with uncertainty. Then the bedroom door opened again and Ted walked out carrying folded sheets in his hands and handed them to me.

"Here, they're clean. That should do it. Good night." He turned around again and walked straight into his bedroom and closed the door. I held the sheets in my hand, speechless, wondering what I should do next.

I looked around the room studying every detail from the imitation pine wood entertainment centre, to the nineteen-inch outdated color television. The walls, dingy and narrow, barely accommodated the obsolete and soiled furniture in the room. Then a familiar sensation came over me.....

"Damn it. I said under my breath. "I have to go to the bathroom." I stumbled around in the dark, reached the house and tried not to look around. I was in and out quickly and straight back in the trailer.

The next morning the sun's rays came flooding in, filling the room with light as I lay there, wondering how soon the little brown eyed boy would be back to reclaim his sofa and television. I lay in quiet anticipation of what to expect.

After looking at my watch several times I wondered how much longer it would be before all Ted's children would come storming in. But no one came. Then I wondered how long it would take for Ted to wakeup, but after an hour I decided I should get up, shower and prepare for the day.

Finding the bathroom the night before was peculiar and a mystery. There had been barely enough light to guide me to the front entrance of the house.

This time it was day, and my journey to the bathroom, although easier to see where I was going, remained daunting, with unlevelled ground and stones that had been laid unskilfully to mark a path.

The inside of the house, if possible, was worse – because of all the clutter of toys, clothing and remote controls, you could barely push the door open.

The adjoining room to the living room, where the children slept, was compressed with bunk-bed furniture and motionless sleeping bodies wrapped in blankets and sheets. They remained as still as the first time I come upon them. It was all too peculiar for me.

I took my shower and was back alone in the living room for another hour before Ted emerged from his bedroom, smiling and mumbling a good morning. He gave a nod of approval that I had flipped the bed back into the sofa-bed and prepared it for the purpose it had been intended.

"What would you like for breakfast? Scott, my oldest son, is cooking breakfast for us. He is a better cook than me and does mostly all the cooking."

"I am really okay. I am not hungry at all but a cup of coffee would be great. Thank you." Ted shrugged his shoulders, turned to the cabinets and rummaged through them.

Practically everything in his cupboard was a pre-packaged imitation of some fruit juice or generic substitute of something.

Where were his fresh vegetables and fruit? Shouldn't his natural Native instincts of eating only what mother earth produces compel him towards another type of diet? It then occurred to me that Ted was the epitome of an American bachelor with kids.

"Voila!" he said as he dug out a canister of what I presumed was coffee and began to boil water for an instant cup of java.

'Yuk,' I thought, 'who drinks instant?' I sighed and realised that not only was I social snob, I was a coffee one too. It had to be the Chicago upbringing, and the many visits to Starbucks and Dunkin Donuts that made me the way I was. I wasn't sure how I became who I was now. My dad's family were not coffee drinkers either.

They drank tea and mostly for medicinal purposes. Manzanilla for the nerves and calming the stomach, cloves for energy when feeling tired, ginger for the kidneys and for pregnant women who wanted to speed up their labour contractions, cinnamon for the intestines…the list goes on.

Maybe I should drink tea instead. Naw, I wanted coffee.

Ted continued to fumble around with cups and canisters, while I sat at the table smiling. I quietly hoped he would not do a lot of talking. Actually, as much as his silence bothered me, I preferred it to hearing his voice. I had come to the conclusion that I didn't like him and that he was a complete prick.

What an idiot I was. How could I think being with other Natives would help me understand my culture better? It was a big mistake. What was wrong with me? They are just people like anyone else.

As soon as I came to one conclusion, guilt took over and I thought, maybe, I was being too judgemental. But, it didn't matter anymore. I had decided while taking my shower, that I would cut my trip short. And I would not dwell on the agreement we had made earlier of me staying three days so I could meet others on the reservation.

Anyway, based on Ted's implied comments about not having many friends, the probability of me meeting anyone was probably close to nil.

I did feel for him and his children, though. It was a terrible loss and had to be tough being widowed with children, and living on the reservation. There was no going around it. But Ted was an arrogant jerk that I didn't want to be around anymore so I wasn't going to change my mind.

I had been trying my best to lead into polite conversation but his stares of indifference towards me caused me to remain quiet.

"There's your coffee. Are you sure you don't want anything to eat?" he said flatly, as he slammed the coffee cup on the table, with every hospitable gesture labored.

His abruptness made me blush. I lowered my eyes staring into the brown coloured beverage and took a sip. "Thank you. Honestly, I am fine. I'll just sit here and drink my coffee."

I took another sip and nearly gagged. There were no doubts at all in mistaking this cup of coffee to be the worst I had ever had. It was cold and sour with no help from sugar and milk. It was turning my stomach, and worst, I would probably not be able to finish it. Ted watched me drink his brew with scrutinising eyes. Just as I started to dread taking another sip, I was saved by the rush of children into the trailer.

Ted sighed in frustration. "Come on. Let's go into my office while Scott prepares breakfast for everyone," he said, turning into a narrow passageway and disappearing. I had noticed the passageway earlier in the morning but didn't dare explore. It just looked so narrow that it seemed inconceivable there could be more rooms.

I followed him into a small office of shelved books, old model computers, monitors, and boxes filled with books. He stooped down into one of the boxes, pulled out one of the books and handed it to me.

"This is the book my wife wrote," he said, proudly

handing it to me. But after he let go of the book there was a sigh of regret. I took the book, flipped the pages, studied the cover and found the cover design strange and not intriguing at all.

"May I keep it?" I asked. He smiled and grabbed another book and handed it to me.

"Take this one too and give it to one of your friends. It will teach them something that most people do not understand." I nodded and whispered a thank you, which he ignored and promptly sat down in front of his computer.

I stood awkwardly behind the black sling back chair he had sat himself in, scanning through the pages of the book he had just given me. I was sure he had self-published and by the look of the many sealed boxes of books, his book was not doing very well. I was curious to know what he was doing to market his book and whether he had tried selling his books outside the reservation. And if he had, what happened?

Although my questions were friendly and by no means prying, I felt they might be perceived as such. I asked myself again why I had come. The initial point of coming to the reservation was to become familiar with his work and to become his friend, but there was no chance of either happening. I couldn't understand why he bothered bringing me here if he held so little regard for me.

I released a sigh of defeat, sat down in the chair

next to his, placed the two books down on my lap and contemplated leaving again. I thought I was going to burst from all the indecision, until I could take no more.

"Ted, I want to leave as soon as possible. I am sure you are not ready for me to stay any longer than a day? Can we look at Amtrak and see if we can find something maybe for tomorrow going to Chicago?" Ted looked away from his computer.

"Sure, I'll get online and see what I can find. Or, I'll tell you what, why don't you get on line while I check the kids. Make sure you check trains leaving from Gallup, New Mexico, not Gallup, Arizona. Okay?" Ted smirked, and in a matter of moments he was on the Amtrak web site and gesturing for me to sit down.

I sat down slowly, but before I could thank him, he got up and rushed out the room, leaving me to search through the train timetables. His attitude wasn't what I had expected. He almost seemed relieved. I felt offended that he didn't ask me why I wanted to leave so soon. I stared at the screen and felt my anger rise again. Staring blankly at train schedules, I froze.

There it was, a train leaving at 8:41 in the morning the next day. I was about to purchase it when I stopped. Maybe that time was too early. What if he couldn't make it? I didn't know what the distance was from Chinle to Gallup. I sat in front of the computer waiting for him to return, but after twenty minutes had passed I realized that he wasn't coming back any time soon.

I walked back to the kitchen and found Ted whispering something to his son Scott. When they realised I was standing behind them, they both turned around in indignation.

I stammered, apologising for interrupting them and softly asked Ted to come back with me to his office. He followed me back and stopped in front of the computer.

"What's wrong, couldn't you find anything?"

"Yes, I did but it's very early. I wasn't sure whether you wanted to get up that early to take me to the station."

"That's not a problem. I get up at four in the morning every day. Why should this be any different? Go ahead and book it and I will take you."

"Okay," I said meekly, feeling foolish for not purchasing the tickets the first time. I went back to the website, and booked my train passage. I turned around to thank Ted, but he had already left. Not wanting to go back into the kitchen, I sat staring at the bookshelf.

I probably could have sat exactly where I was until the next day. Then something caught my eye. It moved behind the box of books and scurried behind the bookcase. It looked like a toddler but, it couldn't be. I thought it might be Ted's youngest son but there was no way he could squeeze behind that bookcase. It had to be my imagination.

Feeling more disillusioned than ever, I questioned whether any good would come out of my visit. Not knowing what to do next, I went back to the living room, sat alone on the sofa and waited for time to go by. I wondered again about what ran behind the bookshelf, and could have been wondering for ages but Ted's youngest son came to my rescue.

He plopped down on the floor and switched on the television. I spent the rest of the morning watching 'The Terminator' with him. He was such a sweet little boy. It was obvious he liked me. During the whole film he kept asking me questions about my home and children. The film had just finished when Ted walked back into the trailer. When he saw I had been watching television with his son he scolded him and sent him off with his older siblings.

For the rest of the afternoon, Ted's children darted in and out of the trailer. By late afternoon, they were trying to convince Ted to let them go to the carnival. After repeated pleas by them he conceded by pulling several dollars out of his pocket. In a flash they were gone.

Ted and I were alone, again, which was the last thing I wanted. I would have preferred an evening at the carnival rather than spend another evening with him. He had mentioned that one of his friends might stop by, which oddly enough I looked forward to it but as fate might have it, just as he finished saying it, the phone rang. She cancelled.

Bored out of my mind, it was a relief when Ted insisted we eat dinner. We sat at the table, eating the dinner that Scott had prepared earlier, staring quietly at each fork-full with intervals of smiles and nervous chewing. I had begun to think that the silence between us had become unbearable for Ted, because he stopped eating, held his fork tightly in one hand and simply stared at me with his piercing black eyes. I sensed he thought I was the most annoying person he had ever met. There was a point that the tension climaxed, when Ted threw down his fork and broke the silence.

"After dinner I was thinking we could do some work. Some spiritual stuff, you know, start to channel the guides. I am going to get a notebook so we can write stuff down," he said.

"Okay?" I said, apprehensively. I wondered whether he'd found out what I did before I worked for the schools. Was he testing me?

There were several occasions when we spoke on the phone that I nearly told him about the column I wrote for the papers, and the radio and television interviews I had done. I had hesitated to tell him before because I was afraid that if I did, he would not want to meet me.

Thinking about it all again, I hadn't been honest.

I wanted him to think that I was a simple woman who was searching to understand her ancestral roots, that was all. Not someone who had been writing and lecturing on the spiritual beliefs of indigenous people, maybe this was the time to talk about it.

Ted cleared the table while I took a quick break over to the house to use its facilities. I didn't rush back. Instead, I looked glumly around at the contents of the house wondering why he didn't push the children to tidy up. I couldn't help my reaction to the mess. I was truly a mom in every sense of the word. I understood how difficult it was for the boys to lose their mother and how hard it must have been for Ted to lose his wife; but I couldn't excuse the lack of general cleanliness and interest in making a real home for his children.

I became lost in my thoughts again, remembering the visits to Texas, the laughter, the music, the natter. I doubted there had been much laughter here in a very long time.

Ted's trailer sat so far away from the other homes in the reservation, I suspected, because of this distance, that he had little interaction with most of his neighbours.

I wondered whether living so far from anything and anyone affected his kids. It had to. I felt isolated when we first came off the main road. That sense of isolation surprised me. What did the kids feel having to endure it, day in and day out? It wasn't normal.

I returned to find Ted sitting, staring pensively down at the table, and without warning he began to wail uncontrollably.

"I just miss her so much! The pain doesn't stop. I keep expecting her to walk through that door, and I know she ain't ever going to do that."

I didn't know what to do or say. My first inclination was to put my arms around him and console him, but I didn't dare. I didn't want to take a chance of him misinterpreting my gesture. I stood there, not moving, with my arms hanging at my side. I knew I had to say something. I couldn't be so heartless as to not acknowledge his pain.

"I am so sorry. I wish I could find the right words to ease your pain, but I don't know where to find them."

I patted his shoulder and quickly withdrew my hand. Ted lifted his head, smiled and wiped his eyes. When I looked at his face, it didn't appear to show any marks from crying, making me wonder again whether he had staged his emotional outburst again.

"Don't worry about me. I just miss her. Sorry. She was my soul-mate. We did everything together. We thought we could beat this but we couldn't. We were working hard with our ancestors to beat her cancer. It just didn't work. It could have been all the work we were doing together solving the codes. She solved them, you know. She said that she saw the clouds open up and she saw God!"

Ted wiped his eyes and blew his nose. His revelation startled me. It was all too much to digest. It made me question again whether he knew the type of work I did. But how could he? I never told him.

"We were presenting talks at various centers, when we decided to write this leaflet." Ted handed me a three-page folded document and tossed a few newspaper clippings on the table.

I scanned the leaflet quickly, but it was the newspaper articles that had caught my attention.

Pleased that the articles had caught my eye, he explained, "We did some lecturing on the codes and they ran all these newspaper articles."

"Do you mind if I read the articles?" I said, picking up the newspaper clippings.

"No, go ahead, read them." Ted looked on, watching me read. I thought it was sad that the article was written by a Navajo newspaper and not one with a larger circulation. I felt it could have helped sales for his book. I wanted to give my opinion but I felt a sense of caution. My mother used to say, "Closed mouths, flies don't enter." No one could accuse me of talking too much in this trip.

"It's a good article. Why didn't you go further and run the lecture circuit. There are so many people that would welcome the opportunity to listen to your opinions on life and spirituality," I said, placing the clippings back down on the table.

"Yes, I thought of that, but I am tired of all that now. I don't want to worry about what others want to learn anymore. I want to worry about me and my kids. That's all."

"That's a good way to think. You and your kids should come first before anything else. I know I mentioned to you that you remind me of my family. My dad and I hardly ever spoke to each other. If I really think about it, we barely ever had a conversation unless you consider yes and no answers conversation, although, we did have the one.

"One day he told me he needed to tell me something very important. He had never done that before, so I was curious to know what he had to say. He made it seem urgent, so I sat down ready to listen to this powerful speech he was about to make, "The Indians in Senora can turn themselves into animals." I stopped, and waited for a reaction.

"That was it, that's all he said to me. I sat there dumbstruck. After my father finished talking, he told me to go back to doing what I was doing before and with that, he waved his hand, and dismissed me." I grinned and shook my head at the irony of the whole experience. Ted's forehead wrinkled as his lips tightened.

"And you think what your father told you was nothing?!" Ted angrily got up from the table and stood staring down at me. I felt embarrassed. What did I say? Ted took the articles and book away to the office in the back and returned with his notebook and sat down again at the table.

"Look, write down your experience okay. We are going to try a few things."

"Okay. I am ready, but what experiences do you want me to write down?" I said, a little reluctant.

"Focus, we haven't started yet. Close your eyes and imagine a circle. Can you see yourself in the circle?" I nodded, but found it hard to concentrate.

"Good, now focus. Keep your eyes closed and go deeper into the circle. Further and further, stop and stay there."At first I felt like the unwilling victim of a hypnotism act, and had this involuntary desire to giggle. I tried desperately to suppress it.

I took a deep breath and kept my eyes closed waiting to feel something, but nothing happened. I visualised the circle again and tried to go further but couldn't. I didn't want to offend him so I tried again, nothing. I thought, maybe my subconscious was in conflict with his methods?

"Open your eyes, what did you see?" Ted's face was close to mine, uncomfortably close. I hesitated to answer and clumsily gave my reply.

"Nothing, I am sorry."

"Nothing, are you sure?" he said, beginning to pace around the kitchen table as I nodded helplessly.

"Is this a Navajo spiritual practice? I mean the circle and all?"

"I'm a Scientologist!"

"You're a Scientologist? You're kidding."
Ted pursed his lips tensely. I thought any second he would spit. "I'm sorry. Scientology is cool. I just can't relax."

"I'm not trying to help you relax! I was trying to help you channel the spirit world! Go to bed. It's an early morning."

Ted snatched the notebook away from the table, and marched to his bedroom, disappearing inside for the night. I sat at the table feeling the complete idiot. I gathered my things into my backpack, slipped it by the side of the sofa bed and proceeded to convert the sofa back into my bed.

I switched off the lights and found myself covered in the deepest black imaginable. It made me shiver. It wasn't that it was any darker than the night before, but it felt like it was.

I pulled the sheets over my head, praying that I would fall asleep soon. I nearly did until I thought I heard someone whispering to me on the other side of the sheets.

I jumped, and sat straight up in my bed, straining to see who it could have been. There was no one there, but I could feel someone lurking just in the corner of the room. The ends of my hair stood up, and goose bumps popped up all along my arms.

I thought it might be one of Ted's kids pulling a prank, but I dismissed that idea quickly. They weren't the type of kids to do that sort of thing. They were too serious about everything, with the exception of the little one who was too sweet for pranks.

Get a grip, I told myself. I strained again to see through the darkness of the room and thought I saw the headlights of a car bouncing off the wall. It moved back and forth along the wall and towards Ted's bedroom.

A few moments later there were several more lights, bouncing off his door and wall. Where did all the cars come from? The intensity of the beams increased and was reflecting off the mirror across from me.

Wait a minute, I thought, was there a mirror on that wall? I didn't remember seeing one. I thought long and hard whether there was a mirror, and convinced myself, at the end, that there was. I pulled the covers over my head again and fell asleep.

In my dream the sun was just about to set, and I had been walking for several hours in the desert. I could see the plateau that Ted had pointed out to me when we had first entered the reservation. I walked closer to it and saw Ted at the tip of the plateau, facing forward, erect, with his hands on the lever of a Gatling gun. He held the lever tightly, ready to begin shooting. I waved to him and shouted.

"Ted, I am over here!" But he didn't move.
I waved to him again but he didn't look. He stared straight on, without flinching or moving. Directly underneath him, in a tunnelled pit, I saw rows and rows of stone men standing in a military stance, all in position for war.

They resembled the Terracotta Soldiers of China. They wore breastplates and their faces were transfixed and blank. I stared at them in amazement, and then panic took over.

What if they come alive? I looked down at my hand and discovered I was holding a golden golf club. I examined it carefully and then raised it up, swinging it several times. Confident that I could use it, I readied myself and steadied my feet. I was about to call out to Ted again when I heard a voice calling out to me.

"Bravo, bravo, I applaud you. So, we meet here and again. A gold club, is that all they gave you to fight me with?"

I turned to see where the voice was coming from; standing at the side of the soldiers stood an attractive, impeccably dressed, blond haired man, about thirty years of age. He clapped his hands, laughing at me. I recognised him but I wasn't sure why I did. If so, where?

I raised the gold club up high over my head, preparing myself for the first stone soldier who'd come out towards me. I swung at him, literally knocking his head off. Just as his head rolled off his shoulders, he bent down, picked it up and placed it back on again.

"Oh, Shit!" I screamed. The blonde-haired man laughed harder. I swung again, and again, knocking head after head off the soldiers. They did just as the first soldier had and propped their heads back on. More soldiers moved towards me. I thought it was over for me, until Ted began shooting.

He shattered several soldiers into pieces, but he wasn't fast enough. They all began to storm out, I stepped back petrified.

"Oh. God," I screamed. "I'm screwed!"

My screaming woke me up. Sitting straight up in my bed, with my chest heaving, I was relieved to find that it was only a dream. Nothing had changed. The room remained dark and silent. Everyone was as before, sleeping. I was relieved I hadn't disturbed them. I took a deep breath, and then realised I had to go to the bathroom. But I couldn't go…not alone. I was too shaken up to move.

I eventually fell asleep again, and was up and ready to go at five. I sat staring into space waiting for

Ted when I remembered the lights I had seen before my nightmare. I looked towards Ted's bedroom and then across the wall. There were no windows, or mirrors. I didn't know what to think or make of my discovery. Where did the lights come from? And, why did I think there was a mirror on the wall?

I played out the scene of the lights in my head, trying to come up with a logical solution to what I saw. At the end I decided there was no logical answer.

The first half-hour of the drive to the train station was a quiet one. I thought about telling Ted about my dream and about the lights I had seen but decided not to. My decision not to tell really peeved me off. I hated that I felt so uncomfortable around him.

Anyone would have thought, after allowing himself to cry in front of me, that he had accepted me as a friend?

But his occasional forced smile and lack of interest in conversation with me said otherwise. As we continued to drive along I noticed that we had passed an unusual amount of dead dogs lying on the road.

"Ted, is there always this much roadkill? Aren't they concerned with the amount of dogs being killed on the road?"

"No, why should we be? You sound like this white guy who came to visit the reservation a couple of years back. All he did was complain about the road kill and the way we treated our animals. Why didn't he stay where he belonged?! We get all these Europeans who come here to criticize our way of living!" His voice raised and words spewing, he slowed down his truck and turned to me.

"Why don't you go back to Europe and take all your people back with you! You are just another European trying to be something that you are not!"

His words were harsh and they could not have hurt me more if he slapped me himself with his hand. I felt my tears well up, and I understood why he was so indifferent to me. He didn't see me as one of his people. I was a mixed breed. Lower than the dogs that suffered at the wheels of the car that struck them.

"I have not been rude or offensive to you, please don't be to me." I said as I wiped the tears from my eyes.

I turned and looked out the window. We drove the next few hours in silence. Reaching Gallup I decided to forgive his comments and changed my mood to a more upbeat one.

I smiled at Ted and asked him about the city. Ted welcomed the change and became pleasant and talkative.

Reaching the station, he offered to buy me breakfast. I was grateful and accepted, then excused myself to the ladies' room. When I walked out, he was nowhere in sight.

I STAND ALONE

Do you see my skin?
It's a colour that leaves me in between
I am not black or white
Nor am I a race that others can easily categorize
For that matter "identify"
I have no land—or, really any nationality
So, how can I pledge allegiance to a country
That doesn't acknowledge me?

I cannot pretend that it does not make me wonder
Whether I should pledge my loyalties to another
Yet, my heart beats for a land that was once so sweet—
Clear streams and trees of plenty
Mountains that touch the sky in majesty

It left my ancestors in awe
Refusing to claim it as their own
For this land could not belong to anyone
It could only become their home

FEEDING MY CHILDREN

Then … they came
The land was taken without hesitation
My people were redirected
While they hung their heads in humiliation
As they began their journey of deprivation
Taking on other languages and customs
That separated them from other tribes and nations
No one to say they belong

Even the other red man turned their back on their brothers
Who'd also lost their land to another
Alone they stood
Faceless, becoming ghosts of a history
That would declare that they barely exist

But, years go by and grants are given
Proclamations were made
"Through casinos proof will be displayed that the Indian brothers can be manipulated"
As for me, although ignored, I have endured
And…I still stand alone.

NAVAJO

I decided to stroll around the train station. It was an interesting place decorated in Native American Indian motifs with a restaurant on one side and souvenir shop on the other. I eventually found Ted at the souvenir shop, talking to two very plain-looking chubby dark-haired sales girls in their early twenties.

Ted jokingly leaned against the glass case, winking and pulling at the elbow of one of the sales girls. I self-consciously crept closer to them, embarrassed at seeing such a different Ted.

"So you are Hopi, huh? You're a pretty Hopi woman," Ted said, moving his face closer to the girl who backed away.

"Yeah, and you are Navajo? But you don't look Navajo. You look more like from the south than from around here," the girl said sarcastically.

"I am a Navajo, pure-blooded too... Nothing mixed about me!"

I tried not to listen to their conversation but it was hard not to. The word "mixed" rang in my ears again. I thought; I am mixed. So what! I won't allow myself to be ashamed of it, nor was I going to let his words affect me again.

One of the two sales girls turned their attention towards me and moved away from behind the counter. Ted looked up too, smiled and continued his conversation with the one girl while the other followed me around the shop as I started to browse.

I looked at several Native earrings and bracelets, settling on two pairs of drop earrings. I took them off the display case and made my way back towards the counter to pay.

At this time, Ted and the girls were playing word tennis, ignoring me as I stood waiting. I took out my credit card and held it to catch their attention. I didn't get it. I tried to ignore their giggling at every joke Ted made by waving my card again. One of the sales girls finally turned to look at me.

"That's thirty dollars," she said, taking my card and swiping it. To my amazement, Ted grabbed the earrings from her, put them in a bag for me and handed them to me as if to shoo me away. The girls burst out laughing. He smiled back at them, winked and then strutted out of the shop. It was the final humiliation.

"ALL ABOARD!"

A GHOST THAT DOESN'T EXIST

What do you want from me?
What do you want to see?
Something that existed 200 years ago
Before our land was taken
Before our identity was mutilated

My spirit dwells within this realm of a body
That I can only call my own
I drink like you
But I am not you
I dream like you
But I do not see like you
I cry like you

But my tears are sincere
Yours merely disappear
My heart for others bleeds
But yours perspires like the weeds
That cut off life from the blades of grass
And dulls the rest into a yellowish mass

I love like you
But my love is without restrictions
Your love comes with a list of conditions

What do you want of me?
I cannot be the ghost of a past
That no longer exists
Just to appease your unhappiness.

The announcement came, and not a moment too soon, either. Within minutes I was aboard the train. I had survived my first visit to the reservation and Ted. I looked back to wave good riddance to him and saw him waving back at me with a huge grin across his face. His long black pony tail was flapping upward, with his moustache tipped around his mouth and his dark skin glistening in contrast to his white shirt. Within seconds the train pulled away, and he was gone.

I hurried along the train cars searching for my seat. To my delight my seat was at the very end of the car, and better yet, the car I was sitting in was practically empty of passengers.

What a relief. I wanted to be left alone, if for only a few hours. I arranged my backpack between my seat and the wall for maximum leg space, and realised there was enough space for a makeshift bed. If I was lucky, I could sleep through the whole trip and not wake until the train pulled into Chicago's Union Station. I stretched out my legs, crossed my arms across my chest, and closed my eyes.

The train rolled down the tracks through New Mexico, a state I had always looked forward to seeing. I opened my eyes again, and began to watch the train roll past canyons and towns. It was beautiful. How could I sleep through this, I thought?

Finally, the pangs of hunger overcame my desire to enjoy the scenery, and I set out to search for food.

I walked from car to car until I found the restaurant and treated myself to steak and potatoes. It was a strange choice for me because I barely ever ate meat. But after a few days with Ted and one nightmare of stone soldiers wanting to kill me, it only made sense that the carnivore inside of me would somehow emerge.

I devoured that once living, grazing cow, and didn't feel one ounce of remorse. After finishing my meal, I decided to watch the choices of culinary delights the other passengers made. Most of them ate steak, followed with bottles of wine and whiskey. There were few variations to fish and pastas. I was convinced that people who fly and those that take trains are completely different species from one another.

Train people were the salt of the earth. Plane people wanted fast food and fast solutions. I thought I was beginning to like train people.

A few hours later, I had made friends with these extraordinary people, and joined them in several glasses of wine. At each train stop, I made more new friends. They were mostly blacks from the south who were travelling to Chicago to meet friends and relatives. They made for a jovial group who had plenty of stories to tell.

One colourfully dressed woman in her early fifties was from Haiti. She had met her husband while he was touring as part of the Harlem Globetrotters.

She said she was fascinated by his skill in basketball and fell in love with him the moment she saw him. They married in Haiti and went to live in Chicago. They had been living in Chicago together for nearly twenty years.

The Haitian woman insisted I tell my story as well. I kept saying that I didn't have one and then began talking about Ted and my experiences at the Navajo reservation. Within seconds I had an audience. I was surprised by their interest and after I ended the story at the train station, they all patted me on the back, and went back to their seats or to the bar.

Talking about the reservation exhausted me. I was just about to sit back and fall asleep when I noticed a tall young burly Mediterranean-looking man who was smiling at me.

He sat next to me and introduced himself after the last couple had left. His name was David, an Israeli from a newly built village called Modi'in in Israel.

He spoke excitedly about the newly constructed homes, the clean lined streets and his mother's garden. I couldn't resist asking him why he hadn't stayed. He shook his head and started to laugh.

"I am a businessman. I am here to make money with my cousin," he said, with genuine enthusiasm. He couldn't be more than thirty and studying him closer,

I suspected he might have been younger than that.

I decided not to mention our age difference and let him continue telling me about his adventures in the United States, his political views and his business ventures with his cousin's factory in Gallup.

His cousin manufactured authentic Native American jewellery and shoes. I thought it was strange that a family from Israel would be manufacturing Native American jewellery and I told him so.

"Why is that strange to you?" David asked. "So what if we are from Israel. It's not us who are making the jewellery. It's the Indians who are doing it all.

"That's why we say authentic. We are doing a good thing here. We are giving them jobs, helping them. What more could they want?"

"How much are you paying them?" I said, taunting him.

"We pay them good. We pay five dollars an hour!" David said, smugly.

"Five dollars an hour, how could you pay so little?! That's below the minimum wage. Is that legal?"

"What, that is that good? What are they going to do with more money? They are just going to drink it all away anyway. They are all drunks!" David said, exasperated.

I was becoming frustrated with our conversation

and wanted to change the subject. I grabbed my cell phone to see if I could get a signal, but there was no sign of one. David looked at his, which had reception, and offered it to me, but with a quick nod I declined.

"Are you angry with me? I am telling the truth. They are all drunks.You are not an Indian like them. You are half Spanish. That's not the same. Do you speak Spanish?"

"Yes, I do," I said, slightly annoyed. "I am really tired. Do you mind if I take a nap?" David nodded, stood up and left. Relieved he had gone I looked out of the window and gasped.

The sun had begun to set behind the clouds, casting the most amazing shadows across the land and sky. I grabbed my bag, searched for my notebook and began writing.

"What are you writing?" David said in a low whisper. He looked puzzled and strangely child-like. He was holding a can of coke and in his other hand was a bag of potato chips.

"I thought I would bring you something to eat and drink. Here take it. If you don't want it now keep it for later. I like you. Let me have your phone number so I can call you in Chicago. Maybe I can take you out to dinner or something. I am going to be there only for a few weeks.

"I am picking up my other cousin to bring him back to Gallup. We are driving back. Maybe, you want to come with me. I need a girlfriend." Startled by his unorthodox proposal, I smiled.

"As tempting as your proposal sounds, I think I will have to pass. Thank you."

"Why not, I like you, and I think you like me." I realised my smiling might have given him mixed messages, but I couldn't help myself. I was steadily becoming interested in hearing more about his family's factory in Gallup. But I was too tired to listen, at least not on the train.

"What are you writing? I am curious." He said, smiling again with childlike innocence.

"I am writing a poem." I said, tearing another sheet of paper out of my notebook, and writing my phone number down on it. David took the paper and almost yelped for joy, punching his fist up in the air, as he walked away. He then stopped and walked back over to me.

"What did you say about what you were writing?" David said, leaning closer to me.

"I said, I was writing a poem, about the clouds in the sky."

"About clouds, that's good. Let me read it."

I handed him the poem. He read it, and handed it back to me.

"I like your poem. That's why I want to see you again. I think I love you." David said in a very Partridge Family manner. He tightened the fist holding the paper with my number in it and walked merrily away. I didn't see David again after that.

I decided to sleep, and slept most of the rest of the train journey. When I awoke, I remembered David's food and drink offering; an hour later, I was desperate to go to the ladies toilet. I passed the conductor, who appeared tense, and asked how much longer to Chicago.

"Didn't you hear the announcement? I said one hour!" I tried to politely thank him but he hurried off in a huff.

I discovered later that we had been delayed several times by freight trains, which set our arrival time in Chicago back by several hours. The other passengers were not pleased by this, and had relayed their dissatisfaction to the conductor.

CLOUDS OF NEW MEXICO

Mystical forms appear above the skies
Their transparency allow just enough light
To cast upon them the right hues
To form silhouettes of mountain views
And within a split of a second, they change
Leaving more for our imagination
Clouds transform into a celestial menagerie
Inspiring stirring interpretations
Of the magical New Mexican cloud formations

While in the ladies, I felt the train brake abruptly several times. I rushed to get out and discovered, to my misfortune, several people had begun to queue at the exit door of the train for a quick departure.

I was trapped and no one was willing to move out of the way to let me pass through. There had to have been at least twenty people waiting; all were black. The Haitian woman spoke first.

"We are four hours late! I hope my husband is still waiting for me. Why was the train so late?" the Haitian woman asked as she held her bags in her hand.

"This is all George Bush's fault!" a woman said, huffing and grumbling under her breath. The others chimed in agreement with her, saying the train ride had been too long and too exhausting.

Startled by the outburst, I turned to look at a large buxom black woman in a black top and white leisure trousers shouting from behind several passengers. I laughed out loud. It was the most ridiculous comment I had ever heard.

"How could the delays of this train have anything to do with George Bush?" I asked, amused. I expected others to laugh but instead, the atmosphere became stern and serious.

"Ah, you think it's funny, huh?" the large woman said in a menacing tone.

"What I meant was, how could George Bush have anything to do with the train delays? The tracks this train runs on are privately-owned by the freight companies.

"There was something called 'rail deregulation,' which means the government gave up all responsibility as to who and how the tracks are used. Amtrak is federally funded and doesn't produce enough revenue for the government, so if they are late by just a few minutes, the freight lines have precedence. That's all I meant. Amtrak could run up to several hours behind if need be. The freight lines don't care."

I waited for others to laugh, or at least debate. But the group remained silent, many scrutinizing me with their eyes. I started to feel uneasy and decided to explain my point further.

"Let's say the government could give passenger trains like Amtrak priority to the tracks. That priority had to have been agreed upon before this present administration in order for it to be effective today."

I stood in silence, with no acknowledgment or response to anything I had said up until that point. I nervously continued with my explanation.

"What I am trying to say is the administration responsible for our delays would have been the previous administration to this one, or the administrations before that; they would then have negotiated the terms of the use of the tracks.

"George Bush has not been in office long enough for any repercussions of his decisions to be felt.

"In other words, the responsibility for our train delay would lie on Bill Clinton and his predecessors—"

Before I could go further, a woman forcefully rose to her feet and blurted out,

"No, you didn't. No you didn't say something against Bill Clinton!" I saw her fist rise up in the air ready to bear it down towards my head. Others were shouting and egging her on.

Perplexed by what was happening before my eyes, I instinctively tried to move away but I couldn't. I was lodged against the Haitian woman and the stairwell. Just as the fist was about to strike, a large man's hand grabbed it in mid-air.

"Let go of my hand!" the woman screamed. "I'm sick of her talking all high and mighty, with her fancy words, to Hell with that Bush-loving ho!"

Terrified, and blocked in, all I could manage was to cover my head, and crouch down almost to my knees.

The Haitian woman next to me, having recognized the woman's escalating anger, leaned down and grabbed my hand, trying to pull me up to get out of the angry woman's vantage point.

What did I say? I thought. All I did was tell the truth. The train came to a noisy stop, causing the passengers to reel forward practically on top of me.

The conductor suddenly appeared along with another assistant, pushed the door open, and then laid the traditional stair for disembarking. As soon as they all realized we had arrived, the screaming woman and the rest of the group ran off the train, instantly forgetting me and their anger.

A man who reminded me of John Coffee from the movie The Green Mile was standing before me, grinning.

"Ya really should keep your 'pinions to yoself, Ms Lady," the man said, holding a blue duffel bag in his hand, which he raised over his shoulder, before he walked off the train.

FULL CIRCLE

I needed and wanted the plane to hurry up and take off, especially after our flight had already been delayed by several hours. So, after queuing up behind several tired and anxious passengers, it was no wonder I released a sigh of relief when I finally reached the smiling flight attendants who were busily directing the passengers to the correct aisle for easier access to their seats.

I'd hoped to get a row to myself. I didn't want to spend the entire flight talking to someone who I'd probably never see again. I scanned through the letters and row numbers until I found the seat assigned to me, only to find an elderly Indian woman dressed in a sari sitting in it.

Next to her, sitting in the centre seat, was an elderly Indian man. He was obviously her husband by the way he was holding her hand. At any other time, I would have found it touching to see a couple of that age still holding hands during a flight, but not this time. I wanted her to move. I wanted my window seat.

I gestured to the woman to indicate that she was sitting in my seat, but she ignored me. I held up the boarding pass, and pointed to my seat number so she could move. But she shook her head and turned to her husband. The husband, in turn, shrugged his shoulders implying that they didn't speak English and then clasped his hands tightly, pouted and looked away from me.

I wasn't going to accept an "I don't speak English" ruse just so they could get what they wanted. I shook my head, pointed towards the flight attendants, who were still greeting passengers, and threatened to report them, but they refused to move. I eventually gave up, and found an empty seat at the rear of the plane next to the lavatories.

I sat quietly deep in thought for the next few minutes. I had spent two weeks at my daughter's bedside as she recovered from her surgery, relieved that they had caught the cancer in time. But, as fate would have it, as I was preparing to go back home to England, she received a call to come in for additional tests the day before. It appeared there was still a suspicious mass that required more testing.

I couldn't go back to England without knowing what the test results were -- but she insisted I leave and that everything would be fine. Now sitting on the plane, all I wanted in the world was to be by her side.

The engines began to rev up while I fought to control tears that I had been holding back for several hours. Within an hour after take-off, I had locked myself in the lavatory, crying and hiccupping in between self-

pitying prayers. I prayed for my daughter's life and a positive result from the new cancer tests
she had taken the day before. The more I prayed, the angrier I became, and more tears fell. "The surgery was successful, all cancer has been removed," the surgeon had said while my daughter slept in her hospital bed two weeks prior, recovering from her surgery.

He shook my hand and left the room with his entourage of interns following closely behind. It was supposed to be over. So what gives? I couldn't bear to go through that ordeal again. My daughter was too young to have been diagnosed with cancer in the first place, only to then have the possibility looming over our heads of another tumour being found. It just wasn't fair.

I felt desperate and my mind was going at one hundred miles an hour. I decided to negotiate with God. "God, if you answer my prayers, I will do anything you ask. I will. I will walk across Africa to help the starving. I will help all the children in need in the world! I promise. I promise. Just cure my daughter. Please."

I stopped and wondered if there was a queue outside the door. Had anyone heard me? I composed myself and opened the door. There was no-one. No one had heard. Relieved, I walked back to my seat and immediately fell asleep.

My dreams were erratic and emotional. I woke up exhausted and thinking of God. 'Why should he answer my prayers?'

Who was I? I was no-one special. What have I done to warrant any special treatment? Images emerged in my mind from the daily news reports. I remembered the photos of the woman in Iraq crying and screaming as she cradled her child, wounded from a bomb explosion, in her arms. She was begging God to spare his life.

I remembered another photo image of a Palestinian man screaming for his son's life as the Israeli soldiers continued to shoot at them. The next photo showed him screaming in agony while holding the limp dead body of his five-year-old son in his arms. He had begged God to spare his life. Did God hear him? No.

And, how about those annual charity drives to save the children in Africa who are dying of AIDS. They prayed to God for hope. Did God answer their prayers? Unless you consider the charity drives as the answer to their prayers? I gasped in defeat. I couldn't bear the idea of God not listening.

A sense of longing had come over me, and just as it did, I missed my daughter. I missed the smell of her hair and her warm and wide smile.

How did it get this far? How did I wind up taking a plane back to England? Was it worth it? Were the years away from my children worth it? I couldn't torment myself anymore with worry. I needed happy thoughts. Where were they?

My mind wandered back to the constant flutter of the thrushes and blackbirds who circled outside the garden in Cambridge two years before. Just as it had done every morning when I lived there, I could hear the gentle cooing of the doves beckoning me again to admire the lovely traditional English garden that was just yards away from me.

The memory was so vivid, that I could smell the evergreen near the pond; the perfume of jasmine, dahlias, roses, gardenias and lilies which abounded along with the yellow blossom of forsythia. They were all alive and visible in my mind.

My happy thoughts had finally arrived. I exhaled with relief, and this time tears of joy fell from the corner of my eye. I visualised the sun shining, and it was August again. I recalled my melancholy feelings of knowing that autumn days would soon come as quickly as the summer had. The rain and clouds would follow and replace the sunshine I had grown so fond of. The white and red blooms of the phlox stood erect against the background of fruit trees and the chrysanthemums were ready to bud.

I could feel again the balmy summer breeze that had once gently touched my face and filled me with an array of garden scents. A great calmness had come over me.

ENGLAND

Thunder and storms, darkened skies
that lift my spirit into flight
upon the clouds that blanket me
and glides me along over ocean and seas
to a far-off land, that I had never seen
England

The storm subsides to a gentle breeze
that caresses and protects me for my delivery
You have been waiting; a whispered plea,
anticipating, searching the skies and water
for my arrival, over ocean and seas
to a far-off land that I have never seen
England

There you stand tears in eyes; heart in hand -
for it is true what was told
That a spirit would glide
through the skies, comforted by the clouds,
across ocean and seas

to a land that was never seen
England

I was lifted through thunder & storm, to return your call
to lift your soul, to fill your void
that was left empty for many a year
You, believed in me; that I would come
over ocean and seas from a far-off land
to a land that I had never seen
England

FULL CIRCLE

There was no roaring of the plane engine or the snoring of the passenger sitting across from me. I could only hear the flutter of bird's wings and the rustling of tree branches and the splash from a frog's leap into the tiny pond that surrounded the Evergreen that loomed behind.

He had been hiding behind the leafy folds of the surrounding plants of the manicured lawn. And, if I looked further into my mind, I could see the black ornate gate that led into another area of the garden, where the scent of honeysuckle trailed over the walls and lured you inside to explore an assortment of apple, pear and plum trees.

It exemplified an English garden. A garden and world that was eternal within a country that was England, a foreign land to me.

How did it come this far? How did it come to my reminiscing lovingly of a garden that had nothing to do with me culturally? Everything had changed for me within the last seven years. I had changed. I didn't recognise myself anymore. England had done that. Had I become better for it?

Remorse took over, for allowing England to sneakily pry away my beliefs and customs for all to see and question. Our ideologies and customs had become available to anyone. But was I being selfish, or arrogant? Maybe it would have been better if we had shared sooner if fear of being ridiculed and laughed at had not taken over. But upon reflection, opportunity had never presented itself, until I met Patricia, a girl who worked in a health centre in Southampton.

Her enthusiasm and what I believed to be genuine interest in our traditions and beliefs convinced me to let her become my first student. Once I did, others followed soon after.

I thought that through them I had found home. At the time, it was a breath of fresh air because before meeting Patricia, I had been mugged, spent several months of sleeping on kitchen floors, and in cold bedrooms, and worked at an insurance company that treated pets better than they did their employees.

Southampton was my first harsh reality of the British mentality. Their cynicism and suspicion were a cold dose of humanity.

I had already discovered how the homeless were treated, the people in council houses and the derelicts. But then again, I saw how the poor treated each other. There were many times I felt the England Dickens had written about had never disappeared, but was alive and thriving in every corner and pub in England.

HOMELESS

Where does it stop and where does it begin
Can't you identify there is no truth to your reality?
Doesn't my hardship bring about a tear?
When you walk past me in a hurry to avoid my stare
I stand on the corner day after day
Pleading for coins that you throw away, in a coffee or beer
You ask, "Why don't you get a job?"
"Why must you insist?"
But I try to reply, "No-one will hire a person without an address"
I watch you complain about the injustice of politics
About the wars that are being fought in foreign lands where people are starving
Yet—I stand in front of you barely surviving
Days go by and you see me no more—
You sigh with relief that I am finally gone
"Why do the police allow the likes of me?" you wonder
But it never dawns on you
I have died of hunger

FULL CIRCLE

It was the loneliest time of my life. In order for me to cope, I took refuge in my culture by writing a poem nearly every night.

They eventually added up and led to an evening at an open mic session at a pub. It was an eye-opening experience of standing ovations, cheers and hugs from complete strangers. I had finally made new friends. Southampton had transformed for me from cold stranger to comrade in arms.

It represented a physical analogy that there are never any bad experiences, only learning ones. I guess you could say life had turned into a labyrinth of exciting twists and turns.

The first turn was with my new students. I am not sure how it happened. It could have been my smugness to our customs being safe from thieves of culture and traditions. Whatever it was, it turned.

They began to fight amongst themselves, each accusing the other of not being worthy of learning. One by one they accused me of favouritism. My lack of experience of dealing with such complex matters failed them.

Bitter by their bickering and lack of loyalty to me, I severed all ties to teaching. I justified my dramatics by accusing them of being disingenuous to the teachings of 'Belandu'.

Was I arrogant? Was I as bad as the fundamental Muslims and Christians? I let out an ironic cackle which prompted the passenger in front of me to turn around, just as the flight attendant rolled the trolley down the aisle. I turned down the offer of coffee or tea and opted instead for a stretch behind the lavatories.

I rose with relief from the cramped seats, stretched my legs out and leaned against the emergency exit door. I thought about how much I really didn't understand people.

I couldn't understand why they sought other cultures to understand God? After much debate with myself, I decided God was not the issue. Mortality was. People couldn't cope with the idea of death and what happens after it. So, they looked for easy and fast solutions to explain it away.

I recollected the last gathering at Patricia's home, and the clatter of glasses and laughter from her dinner guests. One of Patricia's male guests begins to sum up a recent experience while the other guests listen intently.

"You see there is a retreat that is held every year in Hampshire by the Daoist monks. After two weeks of meditation and chanting, one of the monks walks in to deliver his speech on what has been learnt from the retreat and how to apply it to life's journey. There were a group of fifteen people busily chatting and sitting around a table. The monk clears his throat to signal he is about to speak, but no one takes any notice.

"The monk coughs and clears his throat again, but everyone continues to talk and ignore him. Finally a mobile phone goes off. One of the followers flips the phone on and begins to talk to whoever is on the other end of the line.

"The Monk, who stood sternly scrutinizing the man on the phone, leaves and returns with a frying pan in his hand and proceeds to beat the poor bloke with the pan over the head. It took three monks and four followers to pull the monk off the poor sod." Patricia and her guests are aghast at the monk's violent reaction.

"That's horrible! How could a monk do that? What was he thinking?" Patricia said, as she shook her head at the other guests, who joined in solemnly.

I, on the other hand, could not stop laughing. The group looked at me, confused and at the same time appalled that I would find such an act of violence funny.

"Isn't Belandu about love and peace?" they asked sarcastically.

"Are you kidding? No. Belandu is about life, and the fundamentals of what makes it exist. Would you take a lion to jail for killing another animal? That would be stupid. Belandu acknowledges all instincts and does not define it as bad or good, or judge its balance and explanation as to what is part of nature, whether it is predatory or human. The monk reacted within that order of human instinct." Patricia coughs and her guests remain confused by my rationalization of the monk's actions.

"Let me ask you this. Was the monk a white British man?"

"What does that have to do with it?" replied the guests, baffled by the question.

"Oh, but it does have a lot to do with it. Was he white or Asian?"

"He was Chinese."

"Ah, I thought so. This man, the monk, spent two weeks teaching non-Chinese people his beliefs and customs. If the room were filled with Chinese, not one would dare speak after meditation. There would be demonstrations of reverence and respect for the monk who has taken his time to teach them. But his white students at the retreat didn't have a clue about what it is to respect tradition. People always want what they can't have - and when they get it, they don't know how to appreciate it. I think it's a rule of life."

A passenger gently tapped me on my shoulder to ask if I was waiting to use the lavatory. The gentle roar of airplane engines filtered back in to my mind, and reminded me of where I was. I shook my head and walked back to my seat, recalling again my last comment to the guests.

"Buddhism, like many other religions, is treated by some like hats, tried on, sometimes as a whim used briefly for a while, and then forsaken and forgotten, almost like a bad lover."

That last comment didn't go down to well. It was met with instant disapproval from Patricia's friends. At the time I couldn't understand why I fell out of favour. But, I realised in time that it was all for the best. If I had remained popular with them, they probably would have converted me into a character from 'The Life of Brian.'

In my mind I could hear them saying that line from the film where the followers are sure they know how to spot a Messiah, having followed a few.

THIEF

Yea, I called you friend
When you swore allegiance to the end
And upon that oath, I heaved my chest
with pride
whilst you stood loyal by my side
My gratitude in prose
you thanked with many congratulatory notes
But "thief" you became, stole my words and
replaced my name
What a vicious deed you preformed
Stole what was not meant to be yours
Is there no conscience? No remorse?
Nay - yet - why should there be?
A person who has no soul, cannot feel regrets
at all
For there is no heart to inspire prose
That you can call your own
"Thief" you became-Not friend...
Or anything.... more

Yes, so much had changed. I wondered if I could make a speech like that again after living in England. The years had rolled by since that fateful walk in Grant Park in Chicago. Steve's voice filled with anxiety as we walked along Buckingham fountain. His eyes, sad and desperate, longing to take back the years he had devoted to his wife and career. I think in many ways I had become his unwilling confidant and therapist.

He was a geologist but worked in management, like me, in the public education sector. As we walked further, I could see the lake ahead of me. Its clear blue waters and clean definition made it easy to understand why a city would build itself around it.

"Feel like walking? You know, if I could I'd walk forever, I'd walk all the way to Colorado if I could. Come on."

Steve grabbed my hand, led me across Lake Shore Drive's frenzy of traffic and took me further away from Central office, challenging the possibility of getting back in time from lunch.

We walked toward Soldier Field and stood in front of the building, scrutinizing its attraction. I felt a slight crisp in the air and pulled my jacket tighter around me. It had been a mild winter, and we had been spared the usual snow storms and bitter falling temperatures.

Remembering that winter with Steve brought on a shiver. I pulled up my jacket over my shoulders and recalled the conversation I had with my daughter, two hours earlier before leaving for the airport. Her voice was low and reassuring.

"Mom, I wish you wouldn't worry. God's got my back."

God's got her back? What's that supposed to mean? How can a mother not worry? I pushed all thoughts of doctors and tests to the side and drifted safely back to that day with Steve.

"Why did that moron change the structure of Soldier Field? You can't improve on perfection." Steve stared in frustration and then scowled. "I don't understand what the idiot was thinking, to allow that grotesque piece of crap be built on top of Soldier Field."

"I agree with you, Steve. It's ugly but I have to admit I don't know anything about architecture, so all I can say is it's a bad piece of work." I wrinkled my forehead and anxiously walked ahead towards the Field Museum, leaving Steve behind.

I felt the urgency to escape. I had sensed the

pending formidable discussion coming, on Chicago's architectural wonders and disasters, followed by feedback time on whether I was listening. I didn't know enough about structural design to give opinions and I hated to be cornered on the subject, just to show how little I did know.

I strode quickly across the empty parking lot, inching closer to the Field Museum's large stone stairs. I felt instantly at home. Just as I started to relax, I felt Steve glide beside me. He walked in rhythm to my footsteps as I climbed the stairs to the museum's entrance.

"Why'd you disappear?"

"Oh, it's just, this museum has always felt like home. You know Steve I can go to this museum a thousand times and never get tired. There's so much to see. It's history, in all its magnificence. I know most people prefer the art museum. Well, I know you do, but I like the Field Museum." Steve slid his arm under mine, and turned me back around and down the stairs.

"Is that what happened back there? I could see you got lost in your thoughts of the Field Museum. I have passes. You are welcome to them if you want them."

"Oh my God, that must have appeared rude. You wanted to talk to me about your wife and I walked away from you." I said, faking guilt.

"Naw, that's okay. Let's walk back. We can talk while we are walking." Steve kept his arm snugly wrapped around mine, slowly leading me back down the stairs.

He paused at the final stair as if preparing for a speech. "I am comfortable when I talk to you. There isn't anything phoney about you. I like your sincerity," Steve said, looking at me intensely. "Do you know what I like most about you?"

"No. What?" I said, amused.

"I feel way deep inside that I can tell you anything, and you won't violate that confidentiality." He paused as if about to say something he had been holding back.

I felt a sudden pang of anxiety. I didn't want to hear what he had to reveal to me. The responsibility of such an intimate revelation was too much for me to shoulder. I rushed off to the traffic lights and pressed the walk button to cross. Steve took a deep breath, and kept beside me, as I made Buckingham Fountain my first target to reach.

"I think we had better hurry," I said, as the light turned green. "I don't want to be late getting back."

"Don't worry, I am always late but then I don't

have a witch for a boss. Pity you. She is a bitch. How do you put up with it? That office is full of hypocrites and back stabbers. I wouldn't be able to stand it."

"Do you really want to know, Steve? Do you want to know my secret?"

"Yes, I do, I want to know." he said curiously.

"I ignore her. That's it. That's my secret. All she ever does is rant, while I just nod my head and do the complete opposite of what she has told me to do. Do you know why I do the opposite? Because practically everything she tells me is a complete lie. So, the opposite is usually the right thing to do. Ironically, and the worst part of all this, she gets credit for all the right things I have done, for doing the complete opposite of what she wanted me to do. Does any of this make sense? Anyway, it doesn't matter now does it? I am leaving this hole."

"Yes, it does make sense." Steve steps in front of me, forcing me to stop.

"That's what I wanted to talk to you about....leaving." Steve's face moved closer to mine, facing me, uncomfortably close.

"You wanted to talk to me about my leaving Chicago? Please don't try to talk me out of it," I said with a tone of desperation.

"No. I wasn't going to. I wanted to talk to you about why you were leaving. To start a new life, right? I want to hear again what you said the other day about being fed up with Chicago, with the United States. I want to hear it again.

Please repeat it because I need to hear it. I need to hear that you are fed up with all the bullshit about race. I want to hear how you are tired of everyone being a colour or a nationality. I married my wife twenty-five years ago, and all I've ever been to her and her family is a 'white guy'; a white father, a white husband, the white guy who married a black woman."

Steve held my shoulders, pressed hard and waited for my reaction, but I paused instead. I could hear the despair in his voice.

"I'm leaving my wife. I want to live in a world where race doesn't matter, and where you measure a man by his accomplishments and his deeds, not his race or ethnicity. I married my wife because I loved her, not because I dug black women. I don't know why she married me, and I can't stay married to her not knowing the truth!"

"Steve, I don't want what I said to you the other day to be the cause of you wanting to leave your wife. I only said it because I was fed up with everyone. It's just that this city…or country is always about whether you are Black, Mexican, Irish or Martian. I am tired of the comparisons of whose culture is richer and better. Who is being discriminated against, and who deserves more. I am just sick of it. I don't want to hear it anymore. That's all I was saying."

"But, that's what I am trying to say. I want to be accepted as me, too. Not as the white guy."

"Steve, I was just letting out steam. I am leaving, because I need to. I can't continue to pretend to work for an organisation that segregates itself from other organisations and pretends to help homeless people, when they keep shutting down shelters. Never mind. We can talk more later after work if you want. I need to get back. I am late." Steve burst out laughing just as I broke free from his grip.

"Listen to yourself. That's right, you're leaving, so who cares if you get back late from lunch. You're free!"

He was right. I was leaving, so why was I rushing back to the office? It felt good to laugh. The pretending and lies were over. I didn't have to watch my boss pretend to care about the people we were supposed to be helping anymore. I didn't have to sneak behind her back and help organisations who relied on our services or families who had been turned away because she refused to approve them for benefits just to keep our budget low. The game was over.

The smell of food had drifted through the aisles of the plane. It made me wonder where Steve was. I didn't think he would actually leave his wife and job, but he did. He retired early and disappeared without forwarding any contact details. But I had a few good guesses where he had gone.... Colorado. That's where he wanted to go, and that's where I was sure he was

I left Chicago because I was tired of the racism and segregated communities, but I was dealing with racism, here, sometimes in my mind.

How does one liberate one's self from the repercussions of discrimination? The injustice of racism is like a bad sore. Left untreated, it festers and becomes infected until it consumes your body and mind. My parents never prepared me for racism. They lived in their world of migration to cities and towns, living among people that shared their views on life and culture. It was as if they lived in a tiny country within another country, separate from the rest...until we moved to the west side of Chicago.

Sleep had finally made its ascent and my mind wandered and settled on the first years that my family spent in Chicago. Sirens of police cars along with shouting and screaming fill the air.

It's 1960 in Chicago's west side. Black Americans are throwing rocks and cans, shouting profanities at the white policemen whose faces are drawn and expressionless, as they escort a handcuffed black man along the streets.

His face is beaten and raw. The white turned red short-sleeved shirt is torn open, and blood is dripping down from his forehead and onto his shirt.

I am screaming and want them to stop. I am only five years old. "They're hurting him, mommy! Those men, they are hurting him!" I sob uncontrollably.

"Who is hurting him?" My mother, confused, tries frantically to pull me inside the kitchen, away from the porch, away from the screams of an angry mob, but I won't go inside.

"They are!" I point frantically at the police. "They are hurting Jesus, they are hurting him! Stop it! Stop hurting him!" I shout at the black man's police escorts. They look blankly up at me and push their prisoner forward.

The black man looks up, blood trickles across his forehead and down his face. He reminds me of the statue of Jesus in the church on Jackson Avenue.

Our eyes fix……locked into one long stare. His black eyes are glassy as they peer into mine, letting me know not to be afraid, to stop crying, and I do. Another glass bottle is thrown into the air and explodes.

The passenger who had been sitting behind me pulled on my seat, having spilt his drink, and I was awake again. He tried to clean up his mess and kept bumping on my seat repeatedly as he did so.

I stepped out into the aisle to give him the room he needed. He mumbled another apology while his wife stared dubiously at me, as he cleared the spillage.

Her stares really annoyed me. I didn't understand her reaction. It wasn't me who spilled the drink. I had wondered whether I had been snoring, or talking in my sleep, to cause her to stare with such condescension.

At the end I shrugged it off, and settled back down into my seat. I thought how easy it was to misunderstand people's reactions and reflected again on the race riots in Chicago's west side.

My parents were not prepared for any of it, but my father, desperate to keep his family fed, would not move. So there we were caught in the middle of brewing hatred. It was a dangerous time. We were in the wrong place at the wrong moment.

I had often wondered whether my dad regretted

moving to Chicago. He must have. We didn't fit anywhere. We were always the wrong colour, culture or race; my poor dad. I'd never really noticed how much he missed our old life until early one Saturday morning. He was sitting at the kitchen table alone, holding something in his hand.

I tiptoed next to him and touched his shoulder. He held out his hand and opened it to show me the limp body of our canary, Melody. I'd never seen my father look so broken-hearted before.

Every morning he'd pull the cover off her cage and she would start to sing for him. He would join her by whistling and they would soon harmonize together. It was something to watch, the two of them.

I thought at first, he had cried because he lost his pet, but I was wrong. Melody's cage represented his caged life and she died in her cage. It broke his spirit and his heart. I decided that Melody made him realise how much he missed the old life. It was a life of clean air, trees and evenings of guitar-playing under the moonlight. We were poor, but we were free.

It was true that I didn't want to live in a city that segregated ethnic groups by viaducts and highways but I didn't leave Chicago because of that. I left because I wanted to be free, just like my dad.

At that instant I wished Steve was sitting next to me so I could tell him about my epiphany. I wanted to tell him that the initial plan for me to move to Spain didn't pan out at all—but it wasn't from want of trying. Would he have laughed at the irony of all my efforts? Would he laugh at how I wound up in England instead? It was the last place I ever thought I'd go.

The plan was for me to move to Spain. At least that was the plan. What a disappointment. Two days wasted with a lot of unnecessary running around. Bad timing I guess is what everyone kept telling me. I had all the appropriate papers and seal in my passport, but the civil servants I met refused to process them.

It didn't matter how much I tried to insist and point out the official seal for entry. They would still refuse to give me the entry stamp and then asked me to leave.

Bad timing was the only thing it could be. New immigration laws had been implemented and the undocumented were now becoming documented and given their residency. Many Spanish were angry. They took their frustration out on anyone trying to relocate. Latin America was the worst place to be from and worse yet if you looked like you might be from there, which, to my misfortune, I did.

"Beef or chicken?" I heard the flight attendant ask the passengers two rows down from me. I had tucked my legs underneath my seat and continued to stare blankly at the seat in front of me. He continued to inch his way down the aisle, until he was looking straight at me, waiting for my answer.

"Beef," I replied.

"Right," he said, "chicken," and placed the meal on my tray. I sighed in defeat and unfolded the aluminium paper to find a very strange looking portion of chicken. I took one bite, gagged, pushed the tray to the side and returned to my thoughts of Spain.

"It's a clear-cut case. You can get a settlement. You should do it. I would." The lawyer who I sought advice from, and charged me a hundred dollars an hour, spoke with conviction.

"Sue for racial discrimination, but you must file this paper first." he said, showing me a paper with official seals on it.

"No. I will not go back on a musical merry-go-round to any government offices again. Forget it."

My head spun, as I recalled being forced to wait, for two hours, in a queue mostly comprised of illegal residents trying to take advantage of the new residency law that would allow them to stay in Spain permanently.

When it was my turn to talk to one of the civil servants, they refused to answer any of my questions regarding my entry stamp.

The helplessness I felt when they ordered me to go to another government office, one of seven offices…I went to them all. It became a cruel joke. The more I thought about those offices, the angrier I'd become. I was so peeved at the end I stormed out of the lawyer's office with these final words.

"You can take Spain and stick it where the sun doesn't shine! I swear to you this; I will never come back!"

But, I did, one year later on from my arrival to England. I had, rather reluctantly, made the decision to walk the 'Way to Saint James' (El Camino de Santiago), an eight-hundred-kilometre trek across France, the Pyrenees and across northern Spain to Santiago de Compostella.

The trek across Spain became a healing process for me and an appreciation of Spain's historical highs and lows. The best parts were the tiny villages where children would run along the cobbled streets beside you, shouting greetings.

Every village I visited was more beautiful than the last, some less friendly but each unique in themselves. Margit, the German hiker I met along the way, was among the more challenging aspects of the entire journey. She could be as dry in her personality as she could be amiable, which drove me crazy at times. Especially so on the night we were kicked out of a monastery at San Juan de la Peña.

What an experience. It was almost surreal. It was a freezing night and Margit would not stop crying. We found ourselves having to find shelter in a shepherd's stone hut, only later to run out of it in the middle of the night.

I could still see Margit, wide-eyed with fright, running down the mountain in pitch darkness, not speaking a word or letting me talk to her for several hours. I suspected it was more then she bargained for in her hiking trip. She didn't want a deep spiritual experience questioning whether another world of spirits or angels existed. But I wanted to ponder it. I needed to talk to her, and she wouldn't let me. We went our separate ways later in Pamplona.

I thought I'd never hear or see her again, until, surprisingly, one day I received a letter from her in Spain. When I opened the letter I found crushed flowers in between the pages with references to how much she enjoyed the trek with me. I was touched by the gesture.

The low snoring of the man behind me reminded me that I should be sleeping, and resting from my thoughts and anxieties. The best part of an empty airplane was no queue for the lavatory. I hated queuing, especially for the toilet, and what was particularly nice was that I was sitting right next to it. All I had to do is get up and step in. But you would think I would be used to queuing, growing up with nine brothers and sisters and just one bathroom.

"GET OUT!" my brother screamed, banging on the bathroom door. "You're gonna get it. Man, are you in trouble. Mom, she won't get out!"

"Unlock this door! Now!" my father shouted. I'm going to give you such a beating when you get out!" I'd giggle because I knew he wouldn't beat me. He never laid a hand on me.

I suppressed an outburst of laughter when I remembered the horrible things I would do to my siblings and parents. I looked down the aisle at the near empty plane and wondered why it was so empty. I had hoped the plane would not be crowded but I didn't think I would get my wish. I very seldom do when it comes to travelling.

I opened the lavatory door, and just before sliding the latch to lock it, I caught a glimpse of myself in the mirror.

I recalled the tapping sound of the other side of the bathroom door in my parent's house. I had been sitting on the bathroom floor against the door for nearly two hours. The tapping sound continued until I nearly fell over to the other side of it. My father had taken the door off its hinges.

The first face I saw was my brother's ominous grin, and then my dad's angry expression. I waited for the beating, but oddly enough, nothing happened. My father simply put the door down and walked away.

I think that hurt more than any spanking. I had tired him out, which worried and confused me.

To me, although not to all of my other siblings, my father was my hero. He loved his children. They were never too noisy or too much of a financial burden. We were his life and he took joy in everything we did.

Although my father loved his children, he could not give up drinking. His drinking had become such a problem, that he would frequently drink himself unconscious.

But in his defence, no matter how bad his drinking binges might have been the evening before, he was up and out of the house at five in the morning to go to work. It might not have been his saving grace for my mother or my siblings, but it was enough for me. I missed him.

I had wished so many times, that I could see my dad and mom again. I couldn't understand why or how they could have both died, at the early age of sixty, from cancer. Worst still, ten years later, my brother would die of cancer as well.

My sense of dread returned. I was afraid. I was afraid of what the tests results would show, and whether my daughter might not be okay. Anxiety took over, and I had started to panic. A draft by the window near my seat sent a shiver down my spine, and I pulled my coat over my shoulders. I remembered that chilly afternoon when my brother and I walked together to the church to speak to the priest. His voice resonated in my mind.

"Cold? Do you want my scarf?" my brother said, wrapping his scarf around my neck as he walked slowly to the church. It was slower than his usual quick pace. His face was pale and drawn, barely able to keep up with my pace.

"No, I am fine." I said abruptly, pulling his scarf tighter around my throat and trying to keep the chill off. "Don't try to be a brother now after so many years of not being one," I said bitterly. I looked up and we were nearly at the church. It was usually a fifteen-minute walk but we were taking longer. I tried to walk faster but looked at my brother and noticed his back slumping slightly and his head hanging lower. I slowed my pace.

"When are you going to let go? I told you I was sorry. Why do you hold on to the past? Let go. Everybody has to move on." he said, almost whispering.

"Move on? Why don't I move on? I can't 'move on' the way you put it. How can I move on? I will move on when the truth is told about my son. That's when I will move on."

"All I am saying…look…I am sorry. We were all wrong. I can't apologize for everybody! Jesus Christ, Gloria! Give me a break! I AM SORRY!" Gino moaned. He stopped to catch his breath and then adjusted his scarf around my neck.

"There, that's better. Tell me about that dream you had, the dream about those people, the dead people." Gino waited for me to speak. I looked into the distance at the big clock on the church's steeple. We were early. Thirty minutes early.

"Why do you want to hear about that? It was a dream."

"Yea, I know, but I want to hear about everything. Everything you talked about on the radio. You know, life, death, cultures. Gloria, I need to hear about it."

"That's strange coming from a devout Catholic. Sort of defeats the purpose of going to see the priest, doesn't it?"

"Why do you like to fight? Come on, tell me!" Gino grabbed my arm and twirled me towards the entrance of the restaurant across from the church and held the door open for me. He walked in behind me.

"I'll buy you coffee. Come on, tell me the stories." We found a booth at the end of the restaurant, keeping the church and clock within our view. The waitress poured coffee into our mugs as I looked out the window. I watched the once-white snow, now turned muddy slush, as it sprayed onto cars and those walking by. Gino stared intently at me, not wavering in his request.

I took a deep breath, first starting out in a whisper, "I dreamt of a forest, similar to the forest in the story of Hansel and Gretel. There was a cottage. I am walking towards the cottage and sensed someone calling my name."

"You 'sensed' someone was calling your name?"

"Shut up, or I won't tell you anything!"

"Ok. I'm shutting."

"I walk up to the cottage's wide wooden latch door, pull the latch back and open it. Inside was a broad-shouldered man with rolled-up sleeves, white shirt and grey trousers. You know the trousers they wore during the 1940s?

"Sitting at a large wooden table, next to where he was standing, was a jovial, robust, blonde woman with rosy cheeks and lips. The man told me that although he didn't find happiness in the previous life he found it in the next, with her. He said other things, but I don't think it's important to go into it."

My brother pushed the coffee away before I could take a sip.

"What do you mean you don't think it's important to go into it?"

"It was a dream. That's all… a dream. Gino, I can't tell you for sure what's waiting for us when we die. This might all be in my head. I can only say one thing. I know…there is something there, or someone waiting-waiting to help us into our next journey. I believe that. I can never forget Rosemary or Frankie when they died. They knew, and I can't explain how they knew."

"That's what I am talking about. They talked to you before they died! What did they tell you?"

"They told me that they were told by angels they would die soon, but I thought it was all in their heads. I thought they were imagining things, but then they died. I felt like a jerk for not believing them. How can you know what to believe anyway? Gino, this is my personal experience; my personal experience to explore, and work out in my head. Is this why you wanted me to come? Was that your real motivation to get me here, so I could talk to you about all this?"

"Calm down. What's wrong with me asking you? Why can't you stop thinking about yourself for once?" Gino paused, and pulled my hand towards him as I tried to get up from the table.

The waitress appeared with a fresh pot of coffee, ready to refill our cups, but they were full. I grabbed my coat and walked towards the door. Gino threw five dollars on the table and rushed out behind me.

White fresh-fallen snowflakes fell, drifting and pressing against us, just as the wind whooshed past our faces, lifting our collars from behind as we hurried along.

"I'm sorry. Come on, let's get to the church," he said, apologetically.

We walked quietly together until we got to the front doors of the rectory. We rang the bell and were buzzed in.

Walking towards the rectory office I could instantly smell the wood polish and frankincense. We were ushered to a wooden bench and waited for the priest to arrive.

We waited and waited. Twenty minutes had passed when a tall, dark-haired man in his late thirties wearing a leather bomber jacket and holding a Starbucks' cup in his hand, came over to greet us.

"Sorry, I am late; Gene, right?" He held out his hand and firmly shook my brother's, then turned and shook mine. He was a Yuppie priest who had been recently transferred to a trendy neighbourhood.
He'd become very popular with the parishioners, especially the ladies.

As we followed him into his office, my brother leaned over to whisper something in my ear. "This guy used to a big-time lawyer and he gave it all up to become a priest." he said with admiration.

"Really," I snapped. "I guess the church made a better offer. It guarantees suckers for clients and offers security."

"Don't start," my brother snapped back.

"It's good to see you, Gene. I hear you are going for radiation or chemo treatment. Is that right?" The priest sat his coffee cup down on a large dark wooden desk, took his jacket off and sat back on a leather high back chair, and crossed one leg over the other.

Gino nervously nodded and looked at me. "Yep, father I'm going to beat this. My sister flew from England to help me recover." The priest looked at me and smiled. I smiled obligingly, observing his smugness as a priest.

"Well, that was a sacrifice, wasn't it? I am sorry that I couldn't visit you the other week. I had other commitments but I am glad to see you are doing well and that you are recovering quickly," the priest said, taking a sip from his coffee.

"It must be difficult to be so highly in demand. Isn't it, father?" I said sarcastically. "So difficult, that you would force a terminally-ill person to come to you rather than you go to them. Starbucks visits are high on the priority list I see."

My brother stood up, pulled my arm and scurried out of the office, leaving the priest sitting at his desk, holding his coffee cup up to his lips.

I closed my eyes and opened them, again. He's gone. I felt a sharp tug at my heart and for a moment I thought I couldn't breathe. I hadn't noticed the stream of tears falling from my chin onto my blouse. I wiped them off with the napkin left behind from dinner, took a deep breath and exhaled.

There was no rhyme or reason as to why my brother and I fell so far apart over the years, but we did. Sadly, time waits for no-one and that infuriated me.

Why did it take a disease to make my brother want me back in his life again? Why wasn't it sooner? It should have been sooner. My grief was unbearable after he died. I decided to do a cross-country trek again, but this time in America. I closed my eyes and I was back.

The Florida sun was blinding. The temperatures hovered over ninety-five degrees Fahrenheit. Hot for an autumn day. I was tired and had been cycling for eight hours, just breaking the two-hundred-mile mark in my trek. I could barely see the men tinkering with their motorcycles that were parked next to the motel where I'd decided to break for a rest. There was no colour or definition, everything looked white and bare.

The voices of the motorcyclists were a baritone of annoying noise and laughter. I couldn't wait to get into my room so I could shut the world out.

The parked motorcycle engines roared louder almost in unison to the rhythm of the wheels of my bicycle as I cycled passed them.

The air conditioner in my room was on full blast, causing me to shiver at first. The last conversations I had with my brother before he died played over and over again as I stripped down bare. I showered, threw myself on the bed, and fell asleep. In my dream, Gino was dressed in his old tuxedo. His white teeth spread into a familiar grin as he stood next to my bed watching me sleep.

"Gloria, wake up, I told you I wouldn't die," Gino said with his usual charm. I opened my eyes and wanted to hug him but I held back.

"But Gino, you did die. You died of cancer."

"No, I didn't. I didn't die. I told you I would beat it and I did. I can walk with you. I am right here with you, ready to walk.

"Yes, Gino, you said you would beat it. You can walk with me now."

The passenger from across the aisle choked while snoring. He pulled at his low cut jeans, revealing more than what I cared to see, and adjusted his seat.

If God is so omnipotent, why can't we get warnings of impending doom?

But maybe I did get a warning about my brother. I just don't remember if I did.

The baying of a dog and the wailing of woman in David's kitchen in Dublin might have been a warning?

We both stopped talking and stared at each other, finally bursting out laughing. But then David, in a strange tone, told me about the Irish belief in Banshees. He said, "When you hear the wail of a Banshee you are sure to hear the news of someone's death."

"Well," I said. "I am not Irish," and laughed.

Then the call came. My friend in Southampton was frantic. She said that my family had been trying to reach me urgently. I felt alarm bells going off and an ache gripped my stomach. She told me to call my daughter. I froze. I was afraid. It was exactly one year previously, in Dublin, that I got the news about my brother's cancer. Surely, it couldn't be happening again.

David held out the phone so that I could make the call. My daughter's voice was hesitant and subdued.

"He's dead, mom, Christopher is dead." My daughter, unable to say more, put the phone down. I stood, holding the phone in my hand, numb and unable to speak or move. David took the phone from me and placed it down on the cradle.

Could that have been a sign? Was I being warned? I knew David was dumbfounded, staring sympathetically at my face while rubbing my arms.

All I could see was Christopher's smiling face leaning against the kitchen door at my parent's home, content with his decision to join the Marines and leave for Iraq. At that time, I didn't think anything would happen to him. My brother, Jesse, wasn't sure.

"What do you think, sis, will he make it? You know, I made it through 'Nam, when all those other guys didn't. What if I didn't pay my debt? What if he doesn't make it? What if he pays my debt for me?"

My brother had paced from one end of the house to the other, frightened and nervous. I didn't know what to say, so I said the obvious. "Of course he'll make it. Those are superstitious beliefs. Get it out of your head, Christopher will be fine."

But I was wrong. The guilt of being wrong hung over me like a bad hangover. My daughter's smile returned to my mind, and I started to worry again. Desperation had begun to build and I wanted to scream. How could fate be so cruel? Today, if I could, I would give my life if fate would spare my daughter's.

At that moment, the plane went through heavy turbulence. I briefly panicked and prayed for a safe landing. Within seconds the plane settled back.

I sighed with relief. It was a point well taken. How quickly we stop negotiating over other's lives when we think we might die. But it was the survival of the fittest. It was natural. The emergency instructions before taking off in a plane proved it.

"Put your oxygen mask first, before your child's mask." It made sense.

Yet, I wondered if I had my 'oxygen mask' on while raising them? I must have.

The moment my children were born I didn't have a clue of what to do. I panicked at first. And then it fell right into place, instinctively. I'd become the Ninja warrior of parenting, with battle scars to prove it....literally.

My children kicked, swore, lied, started their own numbers racket, and sold my phone number to anyone who was interested. Just to feed them was a challenge: I went on dates with guys just so I could bring back the leftovers. I conned them into walking nearly five miles to my mother's for a home-cooked meal, by singing to them and making up ghost stories.

It was a hell of a time but I wouldn't give one bit of it back. None of it! Each tear my children caused me had been returned many times with moments of joy.

Yes, life had been hard for me as a single parent but it was my destiny to battle for my children. It was the way. It was our cultural belief, and culture was life. It was also the preparation to the next world, the new journey so I had been told.

When it's put to you like that, you have no choice but accept the belief of the spirit world, to give reverence and offerings to the ancestors, saints and God, which I have done and continue to do.

But it always appeared to me that my parents' visits to shamans, and then attending Catholic Church on Sundays for good measure, were just a bit of a contradiction in itself. So, what chance would I have negotiating with fate? And what is fate? Is fate in the hands of Gods, saints or angels? In reality, all beliefs and religions have some string of absurdity.

The coughing and the knee pushed forward into my seat from the passenger behind me, along with the gentle nudging of the flight attendant, who wanted to collect my tray, signalled that we were nearly there and I had barely slept.

In two hours we would have landed. I wondered whether my partner was anxiously waiting for me just outside the doors of Arrivals. I couldn't wait to see a friendly smile. The urge to cry came over me again. But I stopped it. I was tired of crying.

"Stiff upper lip," I whispered. How British. Had I begun to think like the British? No way.

The British were too much of a curious breed, for me to have become anything like them. I had been living in England for eight years and struggled to get to grips with how their minds worked. But, I had learned one thing about them. They were a separatist group of people, that didn't like anyone. That was better than being racist. Wasn't it?

Anyway, I shouldn't worry so much about understanding the British. I never understood the Americans either, and I was supposedly American.

In reality, Americans don't understand themselves because they have no sense of identity at all. They are a confused breed of people who rush to Europe to trace their ancestral roots just to prove how white they really are, or not, but am I being too harsh?

Look at the mini-series Roots. While it was on, every white friend I had was constantly apologising for slavery. And every black friend claimed some direct lineage to some African king or queen. But maybe America wasn't worried about proving their roots anymore. Maybe, they were just as fed up with other Americans confronting each other with the question of: 'How American are you?' Maybe they were looking for a way out of being American.

I know I never felt like I was part of any America. The truth is, at least now, America hadn't felt like home for quite some time. Should I have started calling England home? I couldn't help but think of Steve again, and what he had said about his wife. He said, through his whole marriage, all his wife saw was a "white guy."

How did my partner see me: American, Native American Indian, or just as Gloria? The announcement that I had been waiting for blared.

"Please, put your trays away, sit in an upright position and fasten your seat belts."

The plane had begun its descent, and I was nearly home. I couldn't help but wonder whether he was waiting for me near the gate with flowers and a hug? I needed one.

I got a lump in my throat, from the first bump and the release of the landing gear. I always got the impression that every passenger holds his breath, and mumbles a few prayers (which includes the atheists), until the plane is landed and safely on the ground.

The simultaneous sounds of mobile phones being switched back on, after the 'fasten your seat belt sign shuts off, is followed by clicks of seatbelts being unfastened, along with passengers scurrying to get their belongings out of the overhead compartments. It all works in synchronicity.

I decided to wait. I felt in my heart that my daughter was alright. She must be. I needed her to be.

My walk to the shuttle bus was in a dream-like state due to the lack of sleep. I was the last to board. I looked around and found the same people who had rushed to get off the plane seated and waiting for the bus to take them to the terminal. It only proved that it wasn't worth rushing.

I prepared myself for a long queue at immigration and miraculously, when I made it to passport clearance, there was practically none.

As I waited my turn, I scrutinized the different passports of the newly arrived passengers. Why do people immigrate? Why do we have a need to try other countries on? Then turn around and criticise those countries, claiming our country of origin is better? If they were better, why did we leave?

Another miracle, as soon as I arrived in baggage claim, my suitcases were the first to come through the carousel. I wanted to leap with joy. I started to feel like this trip was a "give Gloria a break" trip after all.

I was nearly home at last, and as I got through the doors of arrivals, I was disappointed to see my partner was nowhere in sight. No flowers or open arms. I sighed with disappointment, until I spotted him standing in the queue at the Costa counter, buying me a coffee. I shouldn't have doubted him, I thought. He has always been consistently wonderful towards me. Maybe he did worship the ground I walked on – or not.

We were off, caffeine in hand and back at home in record time. I couldn't wait....to wait. I needed to wait before I could ring my daughter for the lab results, and there was always the burdensome time difference of six hours.

"You're deep in thought, aren't you?" he said, placing his hand around my shoulder. "Why don't you put the laptop away and take a nap?

You are tired and by the time you wake it will be time to call your daughter."

"Yes, I think I will. I think I'm finished typing my thoughts," I said, as my partner closed the bedroom door.

I was dozing off just now and began to dream of my mother working in the onion fields. Her head turned towards me, and she smiled, calling my name.

I woke, startled, and looked around my bedroom. I remembered my mother's words when I asked her opinion of the meaning of life.

She answered, "What do I think is the meaning of life?" in a contemplative tone which I was sure she used to use when she thought my question was stupid. "There has been only one meaning to life for me, and it has always been the same, feeding my children. That's it - being able to feed my children."

It finally hit me, at that moment, what my mother meant and it was so basic and simple. It wasn't about feeding her children. It was the commitment and the unconditional love that drove her to make all the sacrifices she made. And through those hurdles she hoped that her children would follow her examples of sacrifice and devotion.

A pang of longing to see her again, along with various other old emotions, surfaced until a voice interrupted my thoughts.

"Are you okay? Just as you were dozing off, the phone rang. It was your daughter. She called to say everything is fine - tests were negative." The words "everything is fine" brought tears of relief.

"Yes, I am okay. My daughter is alright! Everything is alright now."

I wiped the tears from the corners of my eyes and mumbled to myself, "The true meaning to life is to be able to feed your children."

"What was that?" my partner said, confused by my words.

"I said the meaning to life is to be able to feed your children."

"Right, I like that," he concurred, with a grin and a nod. Then he handed me a cup of coffee.

ECHOES OF MY MOTHER

A familiar sound beckons me near
To embrace what has remained so dear
In my memories her calls were sweet
Awakening yearnings to be heard again
As the desire does not subside
Tears replace the final cry
And, fall they may upon the cheeks
Resembling a face not far from mine
Forever, I shall wait
To hear the sound now benign
Of the familiar voice… that once called my name.

Printed in Great Britain
by Amazon

60994725R00102